THE GUIDE

ECCLESIASTES

D1642776

Gordon J. Keddie

EVANGELICAL PRESS

EVANGELICAL PRESS
Faverdale North Industrial Estate, Darlington,
DL3 0PH, England

Evangelical Press USA
P. O. Box 84, Auburn, MA 01501, USA

e-mail: sales@evangelical-press.org

web: http://www.evangelicalpress.org

First published 2002

British Library Cataloguing in Publication Data available

ISBN 0 85234 485 6

Printed and bound in Great Britain by Creative Print and Design Wales, Ebbw Vale, South Wales.

Whereas other civilizations have been brought down by attacks of barbarians from without, ours had the unique distinction of training its own destroyers at its own educational institutions and for providing them with facilities for propagating their destructive ideology far and wide, all at the public expense. Thus did western man decide to abolish himself, creating his own boredom out of his own affluence, his own vulnerability out of his own strength, his own impotence out of his own erotomania, himself blowing the trumpet that brought the walls of his own city tumbling down and, having convinced himself that he was too numerous, laboured with pill and scalpel and the syringe to make himself fewer, until at last, having educated himself into imbecility and polluted and drugged himself into stupefaction, he heeled over: a weary, battered, old Brontosaurus and became extinct.

Malcolm Muggeridge

Better one handful with tranquillity than two handfuls with toil and chasing after the wind.

Ecclesiastes 4:6

CONTENTS

Page

Introduction 9
How to use *The Guide* 15
1. What's the use? (1:1-2) 17
2. Three facts of life (1:3-11) 27
3. Knowledge numbs (1:12-18) 37
4. Pleasure palls (2:1-26) 49
5. Who's in charge? (3:1-8) 63
6. Eternity in your heart (3:9-22) 77
7. Empty lives (4:1-3) 89
8. The rat race (4:4-16) 99
9. Hollow religion (5:1-3) 113
10. Promises to keep (5:4-7) 127
11. The love of money (5:8-17) 135
12. Alternatives (5:18 - 6:12) 149
13. Hard experiences (7:1-6) 159
14. Clearing hurdles (7:7-14) 173
15. Facing reality (7:15-18) 183
16. Wising up (7:19 - 8:1) 199
17. Respect authority! (8:2-8) 209
18. Coping with injustice (8:9-17) 223
19. Is there any hope? (9:1-6) 233
20. Living in hope! (9:7-10) 247
21. You are only human! (9:11-18) 259

22. The heart of folly (10:1-20)   271
23. Live by faith! (11:1-6)   287
24. Live joyfully! (11:7-10)   299
25. Remember your Creator! (12:1-7)   309
26. Time to respond! (12:8-14)   325
Notes   335

INTRODUCTION

We live in what has been called a 'death-wish society'.[1] Secular man has one life to live, a few short years to 'make it' in life. And he must live according to the canons of a humanism that has no more to offer than materialist comfort now and, if you can make your mark in history, a lustrous place in the collective consciousness of mankind later. While a certain kind of hope attends such expectations for some people, there are many more who see only the prospect of losing out in the end. More and more people are spiralling downward into personal pessimism and feel themselves sinking beneath the waves of a nagging hopelessness about life and the future. That 'death in the city' which Francis Schaeffer expounded so prophetically over thirty years ago[2] has actually become the formative environment for a whole generation. The chickens have come home to roost. The mad slogan of a Spanish Civil War leader named Millan Astray, 'Long live death,'[3] bids to become the watchword of our time. It is, after all, in our time that millions of unborn babies are sacrificed by abortion on the altar of personal choice, convenience and career. So powerful is the impact that some countries are in absolute population decline. It is in our time that schoolchildren are gunned down at random and child molestation is the fastest growing criminal offence. Not least, it is in our time that the scourge of AIDS casts its terrifying shadow across the moral, social and political landscape like a modern version of the medieval plagues!

Most people, however, are not nihilists. There is a very widespread hunger for life and for a happy future. In practice, people who otherwise have no love for God and no hope in the world are still looking for the good life. They just 'keep on keeping on' and leave awkward thoughts about the meaning of it all to a more convenient season (cf. Acts 24:25). But, also in practice, they continue steadfastly to live out of a conventional wisdom that is ever more obviously bankrupt and creeping ever nearer to temporal and eternal disaster. Even the values that order secular society, and energize such optimism as is possible for people who believe that dust is the ultimate and absolute end of every human life, are all built on the shifting sand of the 51% majority — the prevailing consensus of man-centred wisdom. Theologian Alan Richardson was surely correct when he said that 'belief in the objectivity of value is the condition of the progress or even of the continuance of civilization'. Society could not but perish, 'if the generality of men ceased to believe that truth is knowable and moral values binding'.[4] The deepening pessimism of the Western world is a reflection of this spiritual rootlessness.

There are always two ways in which Christians can respond to such a situation. We can keep our heads down, try to survive, and pray that the Lord will deliver us from this awful world in the nick of time (if not before!). This tacitly acknowledges that we believe our pessimism to be fully justified and that God's programme for the contemporary scene is probably less a plan of transforming conquest for his kingdom and more an intention to abandon it to its fate under some mighty judgements.

There is, however, another way. We can illustrate it this way. Over a century ago, two Christian ministers were travelling by train through the north of England. As they drew into Newcastle upon Tyne, one of the men, seeing the Dickensian squalor, remarked that the place was 'ripe for judgement'. The other, however, demurred, 'No, this place is ripe for revival.' In other words, conquest for Christ, as opposed to survival pending Christ's return, is the appropriate aspiration for Christians even in the face of a sad world beset with what look suspiciously like insuperable problems. Where sin abounds, says Paul, grace much more abounds (Rom. 5:20). The Lord marches toward, not away from, the sound of Satan's gunfire! There is meaning, even in this world with all its problems, and it is the gift of God to those who love him and follow him as his disciples.

The book of Ecclesiastes connects with this wonderful and thoroughly biblical notion. Ecclesiastes has been called 'pessimism literature', and therefore a fitting message from God for our spiritually rootless age.

The writer speaks from the contemporary perspective. He questions, even ridicules, the *status quo* with merciless verve. Then having got inside jaundiced minds, he turns their cynicism on its head to point to the only way of meaningful life. It is a masterly *tour de force* — a divinely inspired bait-and-switch apologetic that carries the reader from the edge of hell to the threshold of heaven. It is true, as Michael Eaton has observed, that Ecclesiastes is not a work of 'full-orbed evangelism'. It is 'the opening sentences of an evangelistic message, leading to faith along a pathway of conviction of need. [The writer] asks every man, starting with the same building material, whether he has learnt to cope with his life as it really is'.[5] It is, in other words, a kind of pre-evangelism. The author climbs into the boots of the other fellow — the one who is in the rat race of life 'under the sun' and who feels, in a confused kind of way, that it is 'meaningless' and 'a chasing after wind'. At first, the Preacher muses about it all from the godless unbelieving standpoint and so touches a chord with those who are depressed and despairing over their own emptiness but do not know how lost they really are — or, more important, do not know where to go for some real meaning, some real truth, some intelligible future. Then, as the argument unfolds, the claims of God are unveiled little by little, rising to a climactic appeal to the young to remember their Creator before the decrepitude of age and the finality of death overwhelm them.

In the context of the New Testament, such a message is less than the gospel of Jesus Christ, and yet it marvellously prepares the way for the preaching of Christ as the one whom our Father-God — the Creator we are to remember in the days of our youth (Eccles. 12:1) — has sent to reconcile us to himself through the cross. Ecclesiastes calls us to new life: that life is actually to be found in Jesus Christ, who came 'when the time had fully come' (Gal. 4:4). Because of these truths, the time has come for us to *live* in Jesus our Saviour.

HOW TO USE *THE GUIDE*

Ecclesiastes is one of the first books in a new series called *The Guide*. This series will cover books of the Bible on an individual basis, such as *Colossians and Philemon*, and relevant topics such as *Christian comfort*. The series aim is to communicate the Christian faith in a straightforward and readable way.

Each book in *The Guide* will cover a book of the Bible or topic in some detail, but will be contained in relatively short and concise chapters. There will be questions at the end of each chapter for personal study or group discussion, to help you to study the Word of God more deeply.

An innovative and exciting feature of *The Guide* is that it is linked to its own web site. As well as being encouraged to search God's Word for yourself, you are invited to ask questions related to the book on the web site, where you will not only be able to have your own questions answered, but also be able to see a selection of answers that have been given to other readers. The web site can be found at www.evangelicalpress.org/TheGuide. Once you are on the site you just need to click on the 'select' button at the top of the page, according to the book on which you wish to post a question. Your question will then be answered either

by Michael Bentley, the web site co-ordinator and author of *Colossians and Philemon*, or others who have been selected because of their experience, their understanding of the Word of God and their dedication to working for the glory of the Lord.

There are two other books being published with *Ecclesiastes;* they are *The Bible book by book*, and *Colossians and Philemon*, and many more will follow. It is the publisher's hope that you will be stirred to think more deeply about the Christian faith, and will be helped and encouraged in living out your Christian life, through the study of God's Word, in the difficult and demanding days in which we live.

CHAPTER ONE

WHAT'S THE USE?

BIBLE READING

Ecclesiastes 1:1-11

'I'm so bored!' read the note found with the body of the former movie star. He was old. His career was over. The reruns on television served only to remind him of a lost youth, of vanished vigour and the memory of a place in the limelight. What had seemed meaningful for his life had been entirely transient and had dissolved into the most bitter emptiness. There was nothing left. He was bored stiff by it all. So he 'popped' a pile of pills and died.

Despair is the cancer of the soul. A life without real purpose is a life that is practically over. The contemporary rising tide of despair, frustration, violence, drunkenness, drug-related death and suicide crashes with a morbid eloquence over the empty glitz of Western society and insistently challenges us with leading questions about the meaning of life: 'What's the use?' 'Why bother?' 'Who cares?' 'What is there to live for?' One pre-teenage Scottish girl had her answer to these questions. When being interviewed by a television reporter, and asked if she was worried about the damage her smoking habit was doing to her lungs and heart, she replied, 'Naw, we're a' goan tae die ony way!' So, eat, drink, and be merry, for tomorrow we die!

The meaning of life

The problem of the meaning of life is not new. From the beginning, men have been aware of the transience of life and its achievements. The poet Shelley expressed this gnawing reality in his sonnet, 'Ozymandius':

I met a traveller from an antique land
Who said: Two vast and trunkless legs of stone
Stand in the desert... Near them on the sand,
Half sunk, a shattered visage lies, whose frown
And wrinkled lip, and sneer of cold command,
Tell that its sculptor well those passions read
Which yet survive, stamped on these lifeless
    things,
The hand that mocked them, and the heart that fed:
And on the pedestal these words appear:
'My name is Ozymandius, king of kings:
Look on my works, ye Mighty, and despair!'
Nothing beside remains. Round the decay
Of that colossal wreck, boundless and bare
The lone and level sands stretch far away.[1]

Man's best efforts often look like little more than pretensions waiting to be unmasked. Do the 'paths of

glory', as the poet Thomas Gray observed, 'lead but to the grave?'

Is everything meaningless?

Everyone recognizes that the Bible is concerned from cover to cover with the meaning of life. Deep in the Old Testament, however, the short book of Ecclesiastes presents a specific focus on this perennial question. It is an 'open letter' from God to everyone who is willing to think about the issues of life. In a graphic and relentless way, the awful realities are exposed — and the way is pointed to God's answers. The result is that we have a word, like no other even in Scripture, that speaks to the so-called 'post-modern' society in which we live. Millennia old, Ecclesiastes is as fresh as the dew. The Preacher[2] addresses this message to his own generation with its own particular needs. Even at its height, Israel was, like any other nation, beset with enemies abroad, and threatened internally by moral and spiritual decay. There was more than enough hopelessness and despair in the land.[3] God gave this Word through the Preacher to his covenant people in order to lead them back to the joy of meaningful life in reconciled fellowship with him. The Preacher asked all the basic questions that wracked the minds of men and women in his

WHAT THE TEXT TEACHES

day. And just as surely and as timely, his message impacts on the need of our own day. Is there any real meaning in life? Or is everything meaningless?

'Vanity of vanities,' says the Preacher, 'vanity of vanities, all is vanity' (1:2). This is a classic *cri de coeur* — the plea of a heart that feels itself sinking in a quagmire of frustration and impeding doom. The accumulated despair of the whole world seems to well up within his soul. He feels what they ought to feel. He expresses the pain that they suppress. It is as if he just cannot take it anymore. He must bring men and women to their senses. Do they not see? Why do they go on pretending that their miserable earthbound lives are meaningful? It is all a meaningless charade!

On the face of it, the writer seems to be promoting the idea that everything really is meaningless. We must remember, however, that he is constructing an argument designed to lead us from one way of thinking to another that is radically different. He therefore starts with the *wrong* idea so that he may lead us to the *right* one. He means to expose what we nowadays call the *secular* view of life: a life without any absolutes, a life without the certainties of the revelation of God's Word, a life lived out of values generated by man without reference to God, a life that expects lasting satisfaction from earthbound things. He wants to show how such a life can only be meaningless and must end in disillusionment in time, not to mention eternity. To heighten the drama of his argument, he gives a vivid presentation of this position as if it is all there is!

Surprisingly perhaps, this theme of meaning-lessness is only a means to his primary goal. Later, as he develops his argument, he shows his readers that there is real meaning in life and that it consists in loving God and being his disciples (12:13-14). He is not a cynic. He firmly believes that all meaning comes from the infinite, personal God who has revealed himself to humanity in his Word. Consequently, he is persuaded that this meaning is only understood and grasped in a personal relationship with God —

'Man's search for meaning'

Victor Frankl, a Nazi death camp survivor, wrote a short book with this title, proposing a philosophy of **'tragic optimism'*** as an answer to the problem. Humanity, he says, faces a 'tragic triad' of pain, guilt and death. These should be faced squarely so as to transform them, respectively, into the occasions of achievement, change and incentive for exercising responsibility. The only alternative is to be crushed by these miseries. What this boils down to, however, is a theory of meaning we might call 'making the best of a bad job, under the sun'. Can you think of other common approaches to finding meaning in life, that are also 'under the sun' in their approach?

*V. Frankl, *Man's Search for Meaning* (Boston: Beacon Press, 1992, pp.1391ff.)

a living faith in him, which results in a commitment to discipleship as a child of God.

For this reason we must define our terms carefully. What does the Preacher mean when he ascribes meaninglessness to everything? He is not talking in academic jargon to an audience of professional philosophers; he is, rather, addressing the everyday perceptions of thinking men and women. His point of contact with everyone who reads his words is their everyday experience of life. Everything around us reminds us of our transient foothold on planet Earth, and only a faith that sees beyond this level of reality can find comfort and security, or even meaning itself, that transcend the inevitabilities of change, decay and death.

The Hebrew word *hebel* is used no fewer than thirty-six times in Ecclesiastes. It basically means 'wind' or 'breath', but, depending upon the specific context, it implies vanity, senselessness, transitoriness and meaninglessness.[4] This sense of futility attaches to just about every aspect of our lives: pleasure (2:1-2); property (2:4); knowledge (2:12-16); wealth (2:8; 5:8-15); work (2:17-23); success (4:13-16); youth (11:10); and, needless to say, frustration (4:4,7-8), loneliness (4:9-12), and death (3:19; 11:8). Futility is endemic to the human condition and inevitably recurs in our experience. Furthermore, if this life is all there is and all we have to look forward to, then what might otherwise have been occasional attacks of a sense of meaninglessness become the underlying irreducible fact of human existence. From such a perspective, people may live only because they would rather not die — a considerable reason, to be sure, but one without a demonstrable hope or significant goal. But to be without God 'in the world' inevitably means to be 'without hope' (Eph. 2:12). Even if we have a kind of hope in Christ 'only for this life' — that is, a purely existential, psychological pseudo-Christianity that has no actual redemption beyond the grave — 'we are to be pitied more than all men' (1 Cor. 15:19, NIV). This outlook sees human history as a track relay race, in which one generation passes on the baton of meaning to the next. Having then run its course, each generation, like Pheidippides after his legendary run between Marathon and Athens, sinks lifeless into the dust of the past evolution of the species. It is all journey and no destination. The goal is to keep on and, somehow, to discover some value in the process itself. Meaning is inevitably bound up with fulfilling one's own potential now and hoping to leave the world a better place after we've vanished.

Surely this is why pantheistic monism (the belief that the universe itself is a manifestation of God, as in New Age teaching) is increasingly appealing to a godless, futureless generation.[5] If *now* is all there is, you can be sure that as much meaning as possible will be wrung from it. Why? Because there is no other source! But this source is identical to the 'all' (i.e. everything) that the Preacher declares so emphatically to be utterly meaningless!

The unchanging God

Everybody experiences the changes and passages of life. Transience, and with it an implication of futility, clings to so much that we do and so much that happens around us in the world. The Bible brings this out repeatedly. 'For what is your life?' asks James. 'It is even a vapour that appears for a little time and then vanishes away' (James 4:14). The creation itself, wrote the apostle Paul, 'was subjected to futility' (Rom. 8:20). And over against the seeming futility of our fleeting impermanence stands the majestic unchangeableness of the infinite and eternal God and, not least, the promise of redemption. The psalmist felt this very keenly and expressed it most touchingly in Psalm 102:24-28:

> I said, 'O my God,
> Do not take me away in the midst of my days;
> Your years are throughout all generations.
> Of old you laid the foundation of the earth,
> And the heavens are the work of your hands.
> They will perish, but you will endure;
> Yes, they will all grow old like a garment;
> Like a cloak you will change them
> And they will be changed.
> But you are the same,
> And your years will have no end.
> The children of your servants will continue,
> And their descendants will be established before
>   you.'

QUESTIONS FOR DISCUSSION

1. *List the things Solomon calls vanity (meaning-less). And note why he calls them that. Look up 2:1; 2:4; 2:17-23; 4:4, 7-8; 4:9-12; 4:13-16; 5:8-15; 11:8; 11:10.*

2. *Read Job 1:13-22 and identify the root convictions in Job's response. He goes on to wrestle with suffering and despair. Where does he find hope and final comfort? See Job 19:25-26; 42:1-6.*

CHAPTER TWO

THREE FACTS
OF LIFE

LOOK IT UP

BIBLE READING

Ecclesiastes 1:3-11

INTRODUCTION

Strong statements always engender decisive response: people either think hard or they walk away ... fast! Before we can reject his dramatic proposition out of hand as, perhaps, the raving of a disturbed personality, the writer confronts us with a very down-to-earth question: 'What profit has a man from all his labour in which he toils under the sun?' (1:3). The key expression is *under the sun*. Used twenty-five times in Ecclesiastes, this phrase characterizes the secular life as seen through the Preacher's eyes. And what does it mean? Just that a life limited to material, earthly categories — a life without the eternal dimension and the ultimate reality of the infinite, personal God — is a life lived 'under the sun' from beginning to end. What you see is what you get! Nothing more ... but, sometimes, a lot less! Ask yourself, then, what can be gained in living a life only under the sun.

Many people, like the miner in the song, feel their lives to be another case of 'Sixteen tons, and what do you get? Another day older and deeper in debt.' For every 'winner' in this life, there are multitudes who think of themselves as 'losers' and are assailed daily with a deep sense of discontent and declining expectations. If material or career advancement is the measure of human self-worth and of the meaning of life and labour, how can it be any other way? What we can *gain* becomes the only conceivable palliative to a short life that ends in the dusty anonymity of the grave. Such a feeling of well-being may be no more than an existential moment of comfort and meaning — akin, perhaps, to the proverbially sumptuous last meal of the condemned prisoner prior to his execution. But take it away and you take away the only reason some people have for living! Jesus pointedly asks us, 'For what will it profit a man if he gains the whole world, and loses his own soul?' (Mark 8:36). Modern secular man replies, 'What use is my soul, if I can't have even a little piece of this world?' For him, there is only that which is under the sun. He therefore cannot see the point that Jesus is making. He aches for satisfaction and lasting achievement but is confronted by the same disturbing facts of life at every turn.

FACT 1— Some day you will die! (1:4-7)

'One generation passes away, and another generation comes; but the earth abides forever' (1:4). Even against the measure of the planet Earth and the elements, never

mind eternity, we are here today and gone to-morrow. If you want evidence, just consider the very sun under which you live. The sun, the wind and the streams continue to function day after day, generation after generation. Finite as the natural world is, it might as well be eternal compared to the life span of a human being. Life is incontrovertibly short. Like Paul Baümer, the hero of Erich Maria Remarque's novel, *All Quiet on the Western Front*, we all live on 'the borders of death'.[1] The great expanse of the creation around us is a constant proof of our frailty and our transience. It 'is appointed for men to die once, but after this the judgment' (Heb. 9:27).

FACT 2 — Where is there any satisfaction? (1:8)

'All things are full of labour; man cannot express it.' If all we have are our senses — what we see and hear — we know that there is no end to the round of pleasing them. Just as our eyes and ears demand to be fed with new sensations, so an under-the-sun life is never satisfied. Yet the modern consumer society is largely built on this frantic foundation! From the minarets of Madison Avenue to the hoardings and television commercials of the nation's media-ways, it cries, 'There is no god but Consumption, and the

Admen are his prophets!' For all the glossy promises, it remains a fact of experience that the highest sensations of the cult of consumerism tend to leave an aftertaste of dissatisfaction and a craving for newer and better experiences. Nowhere has this been more evident than in the rise of the drug culture. A whole generation, jaded and repelled by the emptiness of their parents' materialism, turned for satisfaction to the joys of marijuana, LSD, and sexual freedom. The Rolling Stones' epochal hit of June 1965, '(I Can't Get No) Satisfaction', took what had hitherto been thought and insinuated, and blasted it out brazenly as the only way to go! 'There they stood,' writes Davin Seay, 'bad boy superstars seeping disdain ... hammering out a thundering slab of pig-iron rock 'n' roll, drenched with ... not innuendo, not smirking entendre ... but upfront sexual frustration as a metaphor for the whole appalling specter of a bite-the-hand-that-feeds-'em youth revolt.'[2] Drug deaths and the AIDS plague have bitten deep into the now middle-aged 'sixties youthquake', but the frustration only deepens. There is no lasting satisfaction under the sun.

FACT 3 — What's really new anymore? (1:9-11)

From my six years in George Heriot's School, Edinburgh, Scotland, I can recall vividly two of the many things that our Religious Education teacher, Rev. Joe Graham, attempted to teach us. One was the story of

his theological college classmate, Eric Liddell, the Scottish missionary and 1924 Olympic champion at 400 metres, and more recently the hero of the movie, *Chariots of Fire*. 'Holy Joe', as Mr Graham was inevitably nicknamed, waxed unforgettably eloquent when telling of his famous friend. *There* was a man who had life in its proper biblical proportion and who counted faithfulness to God of greater value than even an Olympic 100 metre gold medal!

The other memorable point was about sin. 'Sin', said Holy Joe, 'is first novelty, then

No place for God?

1. Ravi Zacharias has written: 'Apart from God, chaos is the norm: with God, the hungers of the mind and heart find their fulfilment.'* Watch for examples in newspapers and TV, from politicians and teachers, that indicate that the meaning of life is being sought in **autonomy from God**. Start a file of significant quotations.
2. As you read your Bible and assess what is going on in the world, identify the consequences of the exclusion of God and his Word from private life and public policy, and ask God to open blind eyes and bring every thought captive to Christ (2 Cor. 10:5).

* R. Zacharias, *Can Man live without God* (Dallas, TX: 1994), p. 179

drudgery, and finally slavery.' I have never forgotten that, probably because I have found it, from bitter experience, to be such a melancholy truth. And what is true of sin is true of life in general, as lived under the sun. There really is 'nothing new under the sun' (1:9). In other words, what is new never remains new; it soon becomes 'old hat'. In terms of the deeper things of the human spirit — meaning and aspirations — there is no real hope of anything different or better. Today's novelty becomes tomorrow's drudgery and seems, in the end, only to compound the problem. The promise and benefits of nuclear physics raise the spectre of nuclear holocaust; medical research into problems of infertility leads into the ethical minefield of abortion and genetic engineering. Today, there is plenty of change, an endless flow of new things. But what is really new, in terms of the things that matter? In the ancient world, of course, there was a certain timelessness to the passing of the years. The original readers of Ecclesiastes did not generally experience the kind of rapid change that we today find so commonplace and so impossibly difficult to catch up with. The force of the Preacher's words is perhaps blunted by the very pace of modern society. We are, after all, submerged in novelty as a matter of everyday experience. Candid reflection, however, unmasks the illusion. Modern man knows in his heart that if anything has changed, it has probably been for the worse rather than the better. At the root of the matter, secular man views the world and human history as a closed system. There is no God and no divine goal for life or history. All that remains is unaided human effort clawing forward in the context of an evolving material universe. If the new soon becomes tedious commonplace (1:10), the past becomes irrelevant and is eventually forgotten altogether (1:11). History is nonsense. Reality is now. Existence is all. Therefore secular man is unavoidably an existentialist. *Now* is all he has. But now is a bore. What, therefore, does he gain under the sun?

Another way

The Preacher's readers knew that there was another way. They were aware, for example, that God had created the world and declared it to be good (Gen. 1:10,18,21,25,31; Ps. 19:1-6; 97:6). They understood that sin had entered the world and marred significantly its every aspect and operation. They recognized that it was in the fallenness of the world that death, frustration and meaninglessness had their origin. This was the message of Moses and the prophets, who also proclaimed redemption for mankind and renovation of the creation itself (Isa. 11:6-9; 65:17-25). They knew that the Preacher was speaking for God and pointing to a better way.

With New Testament fulness, this promise of redemption comes to the hopelessness felt by so many in our time. The apostle Paul tells us that 'the earnest expectation of the creation eagerly waits for the revealing of the sons of God' and declares that the whole of created reality will be brought 'into the glorious liberty of the children of God' (Rom. 8:19,21).

There is an alternative to meaninglessness. It is to see the world God's way. It is to realize your need of a Saviour and to come to him in the person of the Lord Jesus Christ, whose death effects the redemption of the lost who will come to him. Christ is the focus of all meaning for a fallen world. Life without a personal faith relationship with the Lord — a godless, secular, under-the-sun life — is life without ultimate meaning. It is life without a future. More accurately, it is life with an endless non-future of eternal alienation from God. Such life in the present is without true meaningfulness, however much it is overlaid by the pursuit of knowledge or pleasure. Such life is Shelley's 'Ozymandius' revisited (see p. 19). But Jesus calls us, in the good news of his everlasting gospel, to new life in him — to fulness of meaning — right now and for evermore.

QUESTIONS FOR DISCUSSION

1. What is an 'under the sun' life? Compare 1 Corinthians 15:19 and Ephesians 2:12. What is the problem with this?

2. Discuss the three facts of life set out in verses 4, 8 and 9. How do these contribute to a sense of futility in life?

DISCUSS IT

3. *Is there any escape from an 'under-the-sun' life? What does God say about this world and our life: where it all came from (Ps. 19:1-6); how he views it (Gen. 1:10,18,21); and where it is going (Isa. 65:17-25; Rom. 8:19-20)?*

THE GUIDE

CHAPTER THREE

KNOWLEDGE NUMBS

LOOK IT UP

BIBLE READING

Ecclesiastes 1:12-18

INTRODUCTION

Unlearning something is often a necessary precursor to genuine progress in education. C. S. Lewis saw it in terms of knocking down forests to irrigate deserts. Something may need to be undone before anything new can be achieved. 'Forget everything you've learned in high school,' said our professor to the freshmen chemistry class, 'it's fifty years out of date, anyway!' Allowing for the usual dramatic licence, there is a profound practical truth in this piece of academic boasting.

This, in a nutshell, is the basic method of the writer of Ecclesiastes. He means to break us down in order to build us up in the right way. There is a wonderful illustration of this concept in Glasgow, Scotland. A major hotel had been gutted by fire and plans made for its reconstruction. This had taken up most of a magnificent Victorian terrace, a row of once private homes having been adapted for use as a hotel. The façade had historic architectural significance and could not be replaced by a concrete and glass skyscraper. Rebuilding the outmoded interior was, however, equally impossible, simply because modern facilities had to be provided for the business to become viable once more. The result was a compromise of the best of the past with the best of the present. The stone façade was restored to its original Victorian splendour and behind it, virtually the whole length of a city block, a completely new building was constructed from scratch, to the most rigorous modern specifications!

Accordingly, Solomon leads us down the dark corridors of life's dead ends. He faces us with the consequences of a life that has no place for God. He exposes the depressing realities of life 'under the sun' to destroy our happiest illusions and so bring us, like the lost son in Jesus' parable (Luke 15:11-32), to our senses — and, thereby, to repentance, reconciliation and a life of renewal. That prodigal son had to lose everything before he would face the fact that he had reduced himself to a lower state than the pigs he was employed to feed! He had to unlearn the fantasies that hitherto had been his guiding lights. So, similarly, must modern 'under-the-sun' people come to an end of themselves and begin to listen to what God is saying.

Take another look (1:12-13)

The Preacher, having proclaimed the general theme that everything under the sun is utterly meaningless, begins to speak in the first person. He speaks from personal experience. He is Solomon, king over Israel and considered to be the wisest man in Israel's history (1:12). Who can dismiss his testimony, as if it were

uninformed? In modern terms, Solomon is 'the expert'. He is the man with the most distinguished personal bibliography in the field of practical wisdom, having penned most of the Proverbs and a number of the Psalms. Solomon is Mr Wisdom Literature! His authority is unchallengeable. He says, 'I devoted myself to study and to explore by wisdom all that is done under heaven' (1:13). He *thought* — and he thought *long* — about life. He faced facts and searched his soul. Derek Kidner aptly likens this to the intense personal reflections of the apostle Paul in Romans 7: 'Each of these two confessions has a wider reference than to the one man who is speaking. Between them, Qoheleth [the Preacher] and Paul explore for us man's outer and inner worlds: his search for meaning and his struggle for moral victory.'[1]

The application to you is this: Are you willing to take another look at your life? Face some hard questions? Or do you prefer the warm and fuzzy comforts of your illusions? Or will you drown reality in distractions, denial, or even despair?

Study can be a real drag (1:13-15)

1. This burdensome task (1:13)

Our beloved history teacher, 'Bouncer' (so nicknamed because his name was Stott, like the

Scots' word for bounce), looked at us with a sigh. In his hand he held our exam papers and the results were less than brilliant. 'I've taught you all I know,' he half-groaned, 'and you still know nothing.' We fourteen-year-olds were hugely amused, for in our twisted reasoning this meant 'Bouncer' must know nothing, for if our teacher knew nothing and taught us all he knew, we were doomed to know nothing!

Mature reflection in later life sees another, more humbling, side to these words: the more we learn, the more we see how little we know. Advances in human knowledge and technological achievement have not resulted in a new age of Arcadian sweetness and light for the human race. Knowledge *per se* has not produced heaven on earth, under the sun! Two facts had impressed themselves upon the Preacher's experience.

Philosophers and politicians alike can wax eloquent about 'the quest for knowledge' as if it were somehow exempt from the pain associated with more prosaic forms of work. No one ever gets a postgraduate degree, whether masters or doctorate, on a forty-hour work week! The frontiers of knowledge take pioneering sweat. And like the settlers who carved out new lives for themselves from the Australian bush or the American prairie, the pain often seems endless and the frustration without relief. The work goes on ... and on ... and on! And the questions persist to defy the latest 'answers'. Will there ever be a cure for cancer? What about AIDS? Is our very existence intelligible?

This perennial search is a 'burdensome task God has given to the sons of man' (1:13). It is not that study is a

Knowledge and presuppositions

1. Paul Johnson, in his book *Intellectuals*,* assesses the wisdom of the world in which we live. With his characteristic flamboyance, he examines some representative and influential thinkers and shows how their ideas have been productive of many of the ills of our times. Whether he knows it or not, Johnson is describing something of the noetic effect of sin; that is, the effect of sin on the mind (Greek *nous*), and the way it forms its perceptions and conclusions with respect to God's creation, God's Word and his will for humanity.

2. In 1 Corinthians 2:6-16 the apostle Paul shows that we can know the facts and miss their true meaning, if we do not have 'the mind of Christ'. The 'natural man' is blinded to God's view of the facts because of the prior commitments and inherent moral incapacities of his unregenerate nature and the presuppositions he then brings to his thoughts and actions (v.14). Until he is converted to Christ and the Holy Spirit informs his presuppositions, he will never see anything exactly God's way, but will rather 'suppress the truth in unrighteousness' (Romans 1:18,22).

3. The 'fear of the Lord', rather than education *per se*, is the true 'beginning of knowledge' (Prov.1:7). We are therefore called to be 'casting down arguments and every high thing that exalts itself against the knowledge of God, bringing every thought into captivity to the obedience of Christ' (2 Cor. 10:5). What does this mean for your thinking in every area of life?

* Paul Johnson, *Intellectuals* (New York: Harper & Row, 1988).

drag because it can wear us out physically, even though it can and often does. Neither is study wearisome because the world and its problems are unintelligible in their very nature, even if it sometimes can seem that way. The real reason is that God has placed a burden on us! He has imposed a set of limitations upon us that were not always there. We are subject to a kind of discipline that keeps us down — that keeps us, in other words, from ever being so swimmingly successful that we can bathe in the conceit that we are gods, with exhaustive knowledge and monolithic control over our lives under the sun. The Preacher is alluding here, of course, to the curse that was, and remains, a consequence of man's fall into sin (Gen. 3:17-19). The whole creation is subject to this judicial consequence of man's ethical rebellion against God (Rom. 8:20).

2. Grasping for the wind (1:14)

In this context, the focus is on the unremitting quest for answers to the meaning of life. There is no end to it. Today's new discovery gives way to tomorrow's new problems. This is neither merely a circumstance of human psychology nor simply a cultural or sociological phenomenon. It is a thirst, an inner compulsion, a facet of human nature implanted by God. It aches for answers and cries out for relief. And when it limits itself to an under-the-sun outlook, it comes up empty again and again. The point is that any search for meaning apart from God and his revealed will is bound to

be frustrating — a 'grasping for the wind' (1:14) — because it has the wrong starting point.

What is crooked cannot be made straight (1:15)

The difficulty is compounded because some problems are indeed incapable of resolution. In our scientific age, we expect answers. We expect the doctors to heal our diseases. We expect engineers to build bigger and better bridges and aircraft. The public face of modern scholarship is one of limitless answers to life's practical problems — in time, and with the right funding! The reality is quite different. Where it matters — in human behaviour, individual and social — the darkness remains and even deepens. And the wise men go around and around, as they have for centuries, looking in vain for answers under the sun. What is 'crooked' still 'cannot be made straight' (1:15).

Knowledge, once attained, fails (1:16-18)

A little knowledge may be a dangerous thing, but a lot of it can sometimes be downright depressing. How many times have you wished you knew what was going to happen? Let's suppose you could see the future. Would it solve your

WHAT THE TEXT TEACHES

present fears? It would, of course, remove uncertainty. But, strange as it may seem, uncertainty is not the greatest of our difficulties in life. A far greater problem is that of *controlling our destiny.* That is the true root of our concern with the future and its uncertainties.

Even an ability to predict the future would actually be a dubious asset. Why? Because it could not guarantee any capacity to channel that future to our welfare. A simple example of this would be a situation in which you were tied to a railroad track in the sure knowledge that the 9:30 Express will be on time and you can do nothing about it! A great deal of scholarship — and all occult practices and witchcraft — attempts to make up this kind of deficiency and exercise a tangible control over events. Scientific models are constructed in such a way as to anticipate likely future scenarios and thus, scientists hope, exercise a measure of control over contingencies as they arise — this secular prophetism is called 'futurology'. Bridges are engineered. Diplomacy is shaped. Plans are drawn. Armies are deployed. Such models or predictions often represent considerable wisdom. They may actually influence future actions. But they cannot be said to constitute *sovereignty* over future events in any ultimate and therefore absolutely sure sense. Rudyard Kipling's sombre and prophetic imperialist hymn, 'Recessional', expresses something of that endemic inadequacy of man's best-laid plans. Spoken to the British Empire at its magnificent climax, Kipling's words stand as both warning and epitaph for all the arrogance of godless power.

Far-called, our navies melt away;
   On dune and headland sinks the fire:
Lo, all our pomp of yesterday
   Is one with Nineveh and Tyre!
Judge of the nations, spare us yet,
Lest we forget — lest we forget![2]

If, then, we have no real control over events, the knowledge of what is about to happen will be potentially devastating. More than a mere foreboding of some future threat, it would become a painful awareness of inevitabilities, without the encouragement of some power to influence or change them in a happier direction. As it is, our lives are frequently punctuated by clear knowledge of future experiences — some good, some not so good. Terminal illness can bring the numbering of our days to a poignant preciseness. We feel the trials and tribulations all the more keenly when they are anticipated. And while, with God's grace, these may occasion spiritual victories of the most exalted sweetness, without doubt these are the deep waters through which the soul must pass. Knowing our future troubles is never a thrill. To know them *all* might seem little better than a suburb of hell.

The Preacher looks at his personal experience. He took his thinking very seriously. He was a wise man. And precisely because of that, he saw the realities. Ignorance is a kind of bliss, after all, for 'in much wisdom is much grief, and

WHAT THE TEXT TEACHES

he who increases knowledge increases sorrow' (1:18). It would be a great mistake to see this as a commendation of ignorance, however. The frying pan may be cooler than a fire, but it is no place to build a happy and fulfilling life! There is a German proverb that sums it up with untranslatable pathos: '*Viel Wissen macht Kopfweh.*' This means, 'Much knowledge makes for a headache.'[3] In a fallen and imperfect world, pain snaps at the heels of our best endeavours. But to labour in the belief that we shall solve the problem of the meaning of life, outside a personal trust in God and feeding upon his Word, is to institutionalize futility and clothe our life with the frustrating reality that we may be always learning but never seem able to come to the knowledge of the truth (2 Tim. 3:7).

QUESTIONS FOR DISCUSSION

1. Why did the writer find knowledge and study frustrating? (1:12-15).

2. What light do Genesis 3:17-19 and Romans 8:20 shed on these problems?

3. What do verses 16-18 tell us about the effectiveness of knowledge once it is attained?

4. Does knowledge really help us control our destiny? Discuss Proverbs 27:1.

THE GUIDE

CHAPTER FOUR

PLEASURE
PALLS

LOOK IT UP

⬤ BIBLE READING ⊃

Ecclesiastes 2:1-26

INTRODUCTION

If the failure of knowledge represents the bankruptcy of rationalism, then to turn to pleasure as a solution is to dip into the well of irrationality. Or, putting it another way, when the books don't give the answers, it's time to pass the bottle! 'I said in my heart,' says the Preacher, 'come now, I will test you with mirth...' (2:1). What many do just because they want to, the Preacher turns into an experiment. If knowledge fails, can fun succeed? Is it true, as the modern 'bumpersticker' proclaims, 'He who has the most toys wins'? Can sensual and carnal joy give the lasting satisfaction that he — and we — crave with body and soul? Can *hedonism*, the indulgence of the senses, provide fulfilment and meaning?

Some people seem to think so. An American publication, *Gentleman's Quarterly*, ran an article as long ago as June 1987 about the things a 'gentleman' should do by age thirty. These included, among a list of 99 items, having sex 1,248 times with 19 partners. Commenting on this, Robert Ingram noted that the significant point is that this publication 'not only advocates and endorses hedonism, but also speaks of it in terms of "oughtness" or moral imperatives'. It reveals, he adds, 'an "under the sun" ethical system where God is absent'.[1]

This was the philosophy of the Cyrenaics, a fifth-century-B.C. school of Greek philosophers, who, along with the more famous Epicureans, held that religion (i.e. fear of future punishment for sin) was a burden that ruined the enjoyment of this present life. The Cyrenaics advocated freedom to bathe in the pleasures of the senses, with relatively little regard to the consequences. Gordon Clark wryly records the parody of the Cyrenaic motto: 'Eat, drink and be merry, for tomorrow we shall have gout, cirrhosis of the liver and *delirium tremens*.'[2] For them, real pleasure was the pleasure *of the moment* — the experience of the pleasurable act.

The Epicureans were more moderate. For them, the known evil consequences of sensual pleasures operated as a limiting factor in defining the nature of true pleasure. They principally emphasized the pleasures of the intellect and, being less self-destructive than the Cyrenaics, survived as an important school for several centuries — long enough for some of them to be encountered on Mars Hill in Athens by the apostle Paul (Acts 17:18).[3]

Pleasure palls (2:1-11)

We naturally identify hedonism with the excesses of sensualism — of endless partying and having a 'good

time' — and think of it as a mere frivolity gone to seed. But it is more than that. It is, as we have seen, a strand of philosophy with a most venerable lineage. As such, it is far more than an excuse for having a fun time! It is a well-marked trail along which many generations have tried to find true meaning in life. It is this, I believe, that the Preacher gave himself to investigate. He did not experiment with gross sin. He simply analysed some of the apparently otherwise harmless, or ostensibly productive, ways in which people amuse themselves.

1. Let's have a party! (2:2-3)

Fun and frolic are the obvious avenues of hedonistic expression. Have you ever been at a party and laughed so much that your facial muscles almost cramped up! Even when the jokes kept flowing, but didn't seem funny anymore, you began to feel that your smile was becoming painfully fixed on your face? Fun — even good clean fun — can wear pretty thin after a while. The Preacher is referring to this kind of 'laughter' (2:2 [Hebrew: *sehoq*]; cf. Prov. 10:23; Eccles. 10:19), fine for light relief, but yet another blind alley in the quest for meaning. Furthermore, 'mirth' (2:2 [Hebrew: *simha*]) — the thoughtful pleasure that enjoys good things — secures no lasting satisfaction. The gourmet palate, the connoisseur of paintings and sculpture, the exhilaration of the raconteur's wit … accomplish what? 'The implication of the rhetorical question is obvious,' observes Michael Eaton, 'all pleasures, high-brow and low-brow alike, fail to meet the needs of the man whose horizon remains "under the sun".'[4]

For all that, the Preacher pressed on in his investigation. Lubricated by the genteel enjoyment of the fruit of the vine, he engaged in the mental exercise of laying hold 'on folly' — giving his mind to the widest range of 'what was good for the sons of men to do under heaven all the days of their lives' (2:3).[5] He drew deeply from the well of fun — but came up empty.

2. Culture anyone? (2:4-11)

Creativity and self-expression may also be the focus of hedonistic excess. And what of these deeper, seemingly more durable pleasures? Such impregnably highbrow categories are assumed *ipso facto* to be a cut above a night out at the pub. If the latter dissolves into a hazy memory of happy camaraderie or fades out into the oblivion of a hangover, the former has the virtue of ostensibly enhancing the common cultural heritage of humanity. Creativity has to it an aura of public service. Any potential for self-indulgence can be balanced by a countervailing motive of altruism and a sense of lasting contribution to the common good. And there surely is a legitimate joy in works of creative self-expression. Art galleries, museums, ruined castles,

THINK ABOUT IT

'Life and death'

This is the title of a chapter in *The Confessions of Augustine* (A.D. 354 - 430). He says, 'You seek a happy life in the land of death, but it is not there. How can you find a happy life where there is no life?' What does he mean? Just this, that God created us and our life is from him. But the meaning of life is not found in just being alive in this life itself (the gift), but is rather in God who gave it (the Giver). This sin-wracked, fallen world is 'the land of death'. Our life is short. If we live only for living, soon we die. Shrouds don't have pockets. We leave everything behind. What then? Augustine goes on to say, referring to Christ as the Saviour who gives new life to all who come to him in faith: 'But our life came down to us [cp. John 6:33], and he took away our death, and he slew it out of the abundance of his own life.'* The meaning of life is to live it in the Lord and for the Lord — that is, according to God's purpose in giving life in the first place, and giving new life through Jesus' death and resurrection. As long as we are 'dead in trespasses and sins' (Eph. 2:1), the meaning of our life will elude us. For if that life is extinguished for ever in death to an utter oblivion (or a lost eternity), what possible 'meaning' could it have had? What 'meaning' could have been enjoyed by those who lived it without accepting what it was for and why it was given?

* The Confessions of St Augustine
(tr. John K. Ryan), (New York: Doubleday, 1960),
p. 105.

magnificent palaces, great literature, collections of antiques, well-tended gardens, and the whole vast mosaic of human cultural achievement enhance the quality and enjoyment of life. Even a 'folly' — one of these whimsical and, from a strictly utilitarian viewpoint, useless buildings put up by some mad, or simply humorous, landowner[6] — survives to amuse the tourists and stimulate the local economy in future days. But do these activities, praiseworthy in themselves, constitute meaning in any ultimate sense? Or are they just another overestimated avenue of otherwise impressive human accomplishment?

The Preacher muses about his projects as a great king (2:4-8) and on the fame that they garnered for him in the wider world (2:9).

1. Buildings (2:4)
2. Horticulture (2:4-6)
3. Business (2:7)
4. Wealth (2:8)
5. Arts and entertainment (2:8)

All of these — houses, vineyards, gardens, parks, reservoirs, slaves, wealth, a harem — are the standard marks of a cultured and opulent Oriental monarch, and they were developed to the full. But had even these highest realizations of human potential and aspiration resolved the real questions? Solomon thinks not. In all this, he says, 'my wisdom remained with me' (2:9). He had kept a sense of reality and proportion. His beautiful

things did not strike him as a joy *for ever.* 'To call such things eternal is no more than rhetoric, and nothing perishable will satisfy him.'[7] It was just sweat, a 'grasping for the wind. There was no profit under the sun' (2:11). These efforts, when compared with similar endeavours today, look remarkably modern. In the world of human ambition, there is, in principle, still nothing new under the sun! And it is still true, is it not, that even the most sophisticated of pleasures offers only an illusory escape from the prison of secularism. Aestheticism, sensualism and creativitism end within themselves. What you see is all you get! The paths of such glory lead but inwardly — and turn full circle upon themselves.

Death comes to us all (2:12-16)

Death is one wall that under-the-sun secularism cannot climb. Even the remembrance of those who have died perishes with those who knew them personally. Beethoven may be said to live on in his music, but the truth is that we know the music, not the man. The names and acts of the famous and notorious remain in the written records and the oral traditions of mankind. But outside of these selective and even arbitrary memorials, the good and the bad, the foolish and the wise, perish into anonymity

(2:15-16). Dust they were and unto dust they did return! True, says the Preacher, wisdom is better than
folly, even under the sun. Even the children of Adam
have a kind of wisdom — at least they have eyes in
their heads (2:12-14; Luke 16:8)! But what can it mean,
if death is all there is?

I hated life (2:17-23)

The answer is brutally simple: If death is where it all
ends, it makes nonsense of the journey. Life is little
different from the pirate's walk down the plank. You
call that 'meaning'? Death laughs at all the moments
of our lives. It curses life and casts its shadow over our
work. We toil away in order to sustain a life for its
extinction! Where is the sense in that! And, when I am
annihilated into atomized oblivion, where is there any
comfort in the fruit of my labours falling to another?
There is no satisfaction for those who have ceased to
exist. Therefore, says the Preacher, 'I hated life' (2:17).
In the under-the-sun scheme of things, this is the depressing conclusion of intelligent reflection. How many
cling to life, only because they fear death more? The
objects of our toil become repulsive (2:18). The *future
inheritors* of the fruit of that work become a source of
frustration (2:19). The very *experience* of toil blights
the days and nights (2:23). All these are meaningless,
says the Preacher. An aching emptiness claws at the
heart. The last resting-place of the secular mind is the
aching anticlimax of absolute non-existence.

Answers to pessimism (2:24-26)

Is life itself just a dead end? Are all our experiences along the way no more than polishing brass on a sinking ship? If, in the words of the rock group, The Grateful Dead, we are indeed 'going to hell in a bucket', should we not at least be 'enjoying the ride on the way'? Should we not just say, 'Let us eat and drink, for tomorrow we die'? (1 Cor. 15:32, cf. Isa. 22:13).

The Preacher gives three answers to these questions, and each one heralds a radical change of tone from all that he has hitherto been saying, as he talks about receiving God's goal, gift and grace in our lives.

1. Enjoy life — as God's goal (2:24)

'There is nothing better for a man,' is a recurring theme in Ecclesiastes (2:24; 3:12,22; 8:15). It affirms that what has become a burden ought to be a great joy! The Preacher starts here with something everyone can understand: metaphysics and bad cooking aside, eating and drinking can be a joy. So, he quietly suggests, why take a jaundiced view of these things? Why not receive them for what they are? Why not accept them as blessings? After all, life itself is a marvellous thing. Does it not look to you as something designed to be good and to do good? He does not mention it, but did he intend to remind his readers that God had made all things good (Gen. 2:9)? Had God not repeatedly spoken of his provision of material comfort and prosperity as a blessing? He provides for us 'richly all things to enjoy' (1 Tim. 6:17). 'For every creature of God is good, and nothing is to be refused if it is received with thanksgiving' (1 Tim. 4:4). God has made a lavish provision for us: 'wine that makes glad the heart of man, oil to make his face shine, and bread which strengthens man's heart' (Ps. 104:15). The point of contact with his sceptical readers — more than that, the *schwerpunkt*, the point of breakthrough — is the fundamental fact that we respond to good things with enjoyment. We may therefore argue from that positive provision and pleasurable experience to the meaning and purpose of these things. Life is meant to be satisfying!

2. Enjoy life — as God's gift (2:24-25)

From experience, the Preacher turns to faith — the ultimate reality that interprets our experience correctly. 'This also, I saw, was from the hand of God.' Receiving life as a gift is impossible without receiving the Giver. This is the condition of true fulfilment, according to the Preacher. This reasonable argument rests on the incontrovertible awareness of meaninglessness in the under-the-sun world view. It is a matter of 'no God, no goal'. Mind you, only a very few will out and out admit that. The secular-materialist hangs on with grim

determination to the notion that he really is going somewhere. But we must insist, against his claims: Does this creation not witness to the reality of the God who made it and reveals himself in the Bible (Ps. 19:1-6; Rom. 1:18-20)? Is life not a gift? The language with which we normally describe the accomplished child and the creative crafts-man expresses the theological truth undergirding our very existence. We call them *gifted* individu-als. In our hearts and consciences we know that life is a gift and there is a Giver.

3. Enjoy life — as God's grace (2:26)

God gives true wisdom and joy to those who please him. This answers a very important ques-tion that is a stumbling block to many. On what basis does God apportion his blessings? After all, there are wide disparities in human experi-ence and the demarcation line is not a simple one between the rich and the poor. Discontent and despair cut through both groups. There is no need to resort to the stereotypes of 'humble poor' and 'extremely rich' to explain this. God does not make all his believers rich according to the conventional materialistic standards of the day. What is significant is that he provides and *trans-forms,* so that he is glorified in the praise of his people — which includes every aspect of renewed lives.

There is in this a very positive message for those who feel the icy hand of hopelessness closing in on their lives. Through a living faith in God, there is joy in the simplest and the most complex of life's experiences. Both the eternal love of God that secures that new life, and the newborn faith with which the new believer comes into a saved relationship with God, centre in the cross. Jesus Christ, the only Mediator between God and man, atoned for all the sins of all his people, as their substitute. In his sufferings and death, he despised the shame and satisfied the perfect justice of God. God's love secured the satisfaction of his own justice in sending his Son to die for other people's sins. And the pivotal point for men and women is, therefore, how we respond to Jesus Christ. He calls us to believe on the Lord Jesus Christ that we might be saved (see 1 Tim. 2:5; Matt. 1:21; 1 Cor. 15:3; John 3:16).

The Preacher concludes his challenge with a solemn warning. To the one who rejects his overtures of grace ('the sinner', 2:26) there can only be a darkening prospect. In an anticipation of our Lord's parable about the rich fool (Luke 12:13-21) and other teachings of the New Testament (Matt. 5:5; Luke 19:24; 1 Cor. 3:21; 2 Cor. 6:10), the Preacher serves God's notice about his judgements upon the under-the-sun lifestyle. The fruits of their labours will not be enjoyed by them but will benefit the lives of God's people. Referring to this loss of the blessing that could be theirs, he remarks (and we can almost hear his sorrowful sigh), 'This also is vanity and grasping for the wind!' (2:26).

DISCUSS IT

1. Why is fun and frolic (hedonism) a dead end in the search for meaning (2:2-3)?

2. Discuss the role of creativity and self-expression (2:4-11). Is a thing of beauty 'a joy for ever'?

3. What does the Preacher say about death (2:12-16)?

4. Why does the writer say, 'I hated life' (2:17-23)?

5. What are the Lord's answers to this pessimism (2:24-26)?

6. How ought life to be lived (cf. I Tim. 4:4; 6:17; Ps. 104:15; Luke 12:13-21)?

THE GUIDE

CHAPTER FIVE

WHO'S IN CHARGE?

BIBLE READING

Ecclesiastes 3:1-8

Some time ago, the American news magazine *TIME* used a catchy and effective TV advertisement drawn from a song based upon Ecclesiastes 3:1 and made famous by a group called The Byrds. Illustrated by suitable and beautiful film clips, this song told us that there is 'a time to be born, a time to die … a time to weep, a time to laugh' and so forth. Insinuated between the couplets is the refrain, 'Turn, turn, turn,' referring to the unfolding phases of life. For the purposes of *TIME* magazine, the message was that their publication would keep us abreast of the times. The events of human life as they unfold in all their variety would be reported to us as they happen. If we will subscribe, we will then 'turn, turn, turn' the pages and the births, deaths, laughs and cries will tumble out in profusion to shed their light upon our way. *TIME* will make sense of a myriad of happenings, by editorial selection of the news they deem significant. History will, in this way, be decanted from the great vat of otherwise undifferentiated events.

Meaning will be drawn from the well of otherwise inscrutable contingent factuality! And we will feel informed! Things just happen, but we can make some sense of them if we work at it!

Do things just happen?

The Preacher, however, had something different in mind in writing Ecclesiastes 3. As he saw it, the problem with human events is not merely one of practical journalism — how to select the news to be published. It is not a sorting, still less a packaging problem. It is, rather, 'How we are to understand what we see and hear?' Do things just happen? Are 'the facts' related or unrelated? Can they be connected meaningfully because they are meaningful in themselves? Or is meaning merely what the human mind imposes upon an intrinsically undefined fact? Again, are these facts essentially meaningless and are we therefore alone, to be buffeted about by ultimate unpredictability on every hand, our only comfort being that one day Ph.D. candidates will gain degrees for inventive theorizing about its possible significance?

These are not rarified questions. They are about ultimate realities that touch our lives every day. Events in the world around us always seem much bigger than we are. For example, everybody talks about the weather a great deal. Why? Because weather can so easily alter our plans. The elements expose how puny we are, how tenuous our control of our lives really is. Many other

circumstances beyond our control arise from time to time. 'The best laid plans of mice and men,' said Scots poet Robert Burns, 'gang aft agley' — and we don't need a translation to catch his meaning!

It is very possible to be afraid and to feel very alone in such a world. Most powerful of all, personal tragedies always bid to crush the person who has no core conviction as to the meaning and purpose of the flow of history and no secure sense of who he is. Even the anticipation of future horrors that may never come has sent some fearful soul into a tailspin of inconsolable despair.

Nonetheless, the survivors are in the majority. There is a steely determination in the resolve of the defiantly godless to live out their under-the-sun lives as best they can, given the uninviting end to which their existence, according to their own way of thinking, must come. At one end of the spectrum of self-reliance we have the trembling resignation of those who see a less-than-palatable future but have decided to get on with the job anyway. But at the other extreme is the fervent humanism of a man like the English poet William Earnest Henley (1849-1903). Henley was a friend of Robert Louis Stevenson and reputedly the model for his character 'Long John Silver'. While deathly ill in an Edinburgh hospital, he also threw down his gauntlet before the claims of God in his poem 'Invictus', in the process centring all meaning in a humanity alone in the universe and autonomous from God.

In the fell clutch of circumstance,
I have not winced nor cried aloud:
Under the bludgeonings of chance
My head is bloody but unbowed.

It matters not how straight the gate,
How charged with punishments the scroll.
I am the master of my fate,
I am the captain of my soul.[1]

This is the under-the-sun perspective, played with all the stops pulled out. A more cautious and less brutally analytical person will just cross his fingers, hope for the best, and put aside disquieting thoughts about ultimate questions. But he nevertheless lives out Henley's creed in practice, even if he would baulk at confessing it openly as his faith. And as long as the sun shines and the wine is good, so to speak, he enjoys being the master of his fate and the captain of his soul. The truth is that all anti-supernaturalism has no option but to live that way. But cracks begin to show when adversity strikes. Then a defiance that rests, in fact, on a foundation no more substantial than the words themselves crumbles to a litany of aching emptiness and fearful isolation: 'Why did this happen to me? What does it all mean? I can't understand it. What will I do now? I don't know if I can go on...' These are the kinds

THINK ABOUT IT

of questions and doubts to which the passage under study directs an answer.

There is a time for everything (3:1)

Merely to state that 'to everything there is a season' (3:1) is to imply purpose and direction; to assert the controlling power of an intelligent providence; to declare that God is on the throne.

'The Mystery of Providence'

John Flavel reflects on the tough times in human life and concludes, 'I do not say that God never afflicts His people but for their sins; for He may do it for their trial (1 Peter 4:12). Nor do I say that God follows every sin with a rod; for who then could stand before Him (Psalm 130:3)? But this I say, that it is God's usual way to visit the sins of His people with rods of affliction, *and this in mercy to their souls*.'*

Is God in control, as Scripture clearly teaches, or are we just buffetted about by 'the slings and arrows of outrageous fortune'? How does God deal with men and women in the course of their lives? List the ways he gets our attention. How did he get Saul of Tarsus to take notice? King David? Adam and Eve? What about you, yourself?

* J. Flavel, *The Mystery of Providence* (Edinburgh: Banner of Truth, 1998 [1678]), p. 125.

The Preacher is certainly not saying that it merely 'so happens' that events occur at different times. That would be a statement of the obvious. Neither is he saying that there is a kind of cyclical inevitability to the flow of time. He is not dolefully observing that life goes on according to some rhythm of the spheres. And he is not talking about some human responsibility to live in an ordered and timely way, as if it is in our hands to make something of an otherwise inherently purpose-less existence.

The Preacher's point is the precise opposite of views like these. God, he says, 'has made everything beauti-ful in its time' (3:11). The sovereignty of God transcends the whole life of humanity in the world. In other words, whatever human agency may be involved in all that happens in our lives, these are in fact the acts of God, in which he unfolds his hitherto secret will for our lives. Even the most free actions of men take place within the all-encompassing embrace of God's absolute sov-ereignty. Scripture applies this principle to the most concrete and dire circumstances. 'My *times* are in your hand,' prays the psalmist; 'deliver me from the hand of my enemies, and from those who persecute me' (Ps. 31:15). God declares: 'I choose *the proper time*; I will judge uprightly. The earth and all its inhabitants are dissolved; I set up its pillars firmly' (Ps. 75:2-3). God 'will arise and have mercy on Zion; for *the time* to favour her, yes, *the set time*, has come' (Ps. 102:13). The great turning point of history — the cross of Jesus Christ — is spoken of in similar terms. It was said of Jesus in his

earlier ministry that no one could lay a hand on him, 'because *his hour* had not yet come' (John 7:30). But on the night he was betrayed by Judas Iscariot, our Lord said of himself: 'Father, *the hour* has come. Glorify your Son, that your Son also may glorify you' (John 17:1). Far from being at the mercy of random events, we await the unfolding of 'the determined purpose and foreknowledge of God' (Acts 2:23).

Everything fits into a plan (3:2-8)

Think, then, of the variegated facets of human life. From birth and death (3:2), the Preacher ranges across the life experiences of ordinary people, demonstrating to reflective minds that the events that shape our lives are much larger than any pretensions we might have to exercise control over them. Martin Luther, with characteristic bluntness, gets to the heart of the matter:

All this is directed against the free will of man, and against all human purposes and fancies, but especially against the notion that it is in our power to determine seasons, and hours, and persons, and measures and place; that we can settle how the affairs of this world shall go, how its great potentates shall rise and fall, how joy and sadness, building up and pulling down,

war and peace, shall succeed and take the place
of each other, how they shall begin and end: it is
to impress on us the fact that ere the hour arrives
it is wasted effort for men to think [i.e. speculate]
and their proposals are useless and vain: in fine,
we are taught that nothing comes to pass before
the hour fixed for it by God.[2]

The Preacher's poetic couplets amass an argument
in support of this thesis. Twenty-five centuries on, we
have little difficulty identifying with his evocation of
the universal human condition: birth and death, planting and uprooting, killing and healing, tearing down
and building up, weeping and laughing, mourning and
dancing, scattering and gathering stones, embracing
and refraining from embracing, searching and giving
up, keeping and throwing away, tearing and mending,
keeping silent and speaking out, loving and hating,
waging war and making peace; these touch us, uplift
us, buffet us, exhilarate us, disappoint us, and, sometimes, devastate us. And, for the most part, they happen *to* us. From outside of us, these forces conspire to
lead us by the nose, often against the current of our
fondest aspirations and our well-laid plans!

We most naturally internalize these themes and
mesh them with our personal individual experience.
But as John Donne said, 'No man is an island.' Even
the most personal of events — birth and death — cannot be locked up into the individual who is born or
who dies. A birth is a powerful event in the life of a
mother, of other family members, of physicians and

nurses, and involves a myriad of other people, all before the baby has the cognitive equipment to reflect on its own existence. An intricate web of relationships forms the matrix of all life experiences. The Preacher is not simply concerned with the thought-life of the individual; he is speaking to people who had a very deep awareness of others. Israel was a nation imbued with a profound sense of corporate identity. They were *God's* people — a fact that rendered their increasing under-the-sun secularization an intensely puzzling and distressing phenomenon. That the covenant people of a loving Father-God needed to be challenged about this problem speaks volumes about the distance they had fallen.

The text itself gives more than a hint of a wider, corporate dimension. The most obvious clue, to modern readers, is in the curious words, 'a time to cast away stones, and a time to gather stones' (3:5). What can this mean? Whatever it is, it would not appear to be any immediately apparent normal activity of people today. The answer is to be found by comparing Scripture with Scripture. When Jesus prophesied the destruction of the temple in Jerusalem, he said, 'Do you see these great buildings? Not one stone shall be left upon another, that shall not be thrown down' (Mark 13:2). The scattering of stones represents the judgement of God. The obliteration of the temple and its worship, accordingly, signalled the fact that it had ceased to be the true house of God and its worship had become an offence to the Lord. It was standard practice in Old Testament times for conquering armies both to scatter stones on their enemies' fields to make them unproductive (2 Kings 3:19,25; Isa. 5:2) and to gather stones for the purpose of preparing the highway for the advance of the victorious soldiers (Isa. 62:10).[3]

This suggests that God has given the Preacher a word for the *whole* people of God and not just for individuals in their private lives. Who does this scattering and gathering of stones in due time? God does it, through whoever his agents may be, and he does it in terms of his righteous discipline of his erring people. A closer look at the other categories mentioned unveils that same perspective. God is speaking to his people so that they, his church, may understand that both their afflictions and their times of blessing fall under the sovereignty and faithfulness of the living God. Herbert Leupold writes, 'There is a periodicity about the things that happen to the Zion of God that helps us to understand her state and to know how far the hand of God is involved in what transpires.'[4]

Planting and uprooting (3:2) relate to the history of Israel's deliverance from Egypt (Ps. 44:2; 80:8,12); killing and healing (3:3) have more than an echo in divine judgement and redemption (Deut. 32:39; Hos. 6:11); and love and hatred toward God's people (3:8) have arisen according to the purposes of God (cf. Ps. 105:25; Exod. 13:3). In every case, including birth and death, the language used has both an individual and a corporate application. The words of Scripture are used with great precision. When with careful study we are able to make the connections with the overall flow of the biblical message, we can discern not only the immediate and personal thrust of the Word of God, but the corporate and eschatological dimension that opens up the meaning of the temporal and the eternal destiny of the people of God. The Preacher speaks to the church as a whole as well as to the individual; he speaks to the 'now' of day-to-day life and also to the 'not yet' of God's purposes for his church in the world. He interprets past, present and future and says to all who have ears to hear, 'There is true meaning both in what is happening to you now and in what is yet to take place. God has set the times and the seasons for everything under heaven.' So, if we are tempted to view events and experiences in exclusively secular, under-the-sun terms, Solomon reminds us that, in fact, these same events and experiences take place under heaven — and heaven is the throne of the sovereign God, who makes everything 'beautiful in its time' (3:11). *Don't give 'chance' a chance!* God is in charge of his creation. Our inability to comprehend the often apparently incomprehensible things happening in our world only proves *we* are not all-knowing — that is, we are not God! The perplexing and dumbfounding events in life must be left for God to interpret to us in his time. Meanwhile we may fix our eyes on Jesus Christ as our Saviour, and trust him as our Lord for every outcome, knowing that he will be with us always to the end of the age (Matt. 28:20).

It is no accident that the advice to ask the Lord to teach us to number our days, that we may have wise hearts, comes from Moses, whose career as God's deliverer of Israel from slavery in Egypt began when he was already 80 years old and had been cooling his heels as a shepherd in the Sinai for four decades. While we and he might reasonably assume that his life was pretty well over by that time, the reality was that the God who has a time for everything was ready to start him on the mighty ministry that changed the world. John Knox was a Roman Catholic priest at age 38, in a day when life expectancy was not much more than that, yet God called him in his remaining years to bring the Reformation to his native Scotland. Your times are equally in the hands of God (Ps. 31:15).

QUESTIONS FOR DISCUSSION

1. Does everything 'just happen'... by chance? Review the fourteen pairs of events in 3:2-8.

2. What does this say about your life and 'times' (see Ps. 31:15; 75:2; 102:13)?

3. How were Jesus' times ordered in John 7:30; 17:1; Acts 2:23? How can this be applied to our lives?

CHAPTER SIX

ETERNITY IN YOUR HEART

LOOK IT UP

BIBLE READING

Ecclesiastes 3:9-22

INTRODUCTION

In interpreting the 'time for every purpose under heaven' passage (3:1-8), we have anticipated what follows. Those eight verses never mention God and do not attempt to define their relevance to the overall theme of Ecclesiastes. But nothing in the Bible just hangs in isolation from the rest of Scripture. On the surface there may be an enigmatic quality to the passage, but, as we have seen, the very words that are used shed light on its deeper meaning. We do not, however, have long to wait for an explicit interpretation. And it is introduced with a very practical and searching question.

What do we gain from all this toil? (3:9)

This is a repeat of the first question the Preacher ever asked (1:3). He is a shrewd judge of human nature. When you tell someone who does not share your faith that God is in control of everything, how do they often react? Don't they say, 'Well, if that's so, where's the sense in us doing anything at all?' They see a tension between God's sovereignty, as you see it, and human freedom, as they see it. This is a legitimate question. After all, there is so much evidence that people do what they want, often with frightening consequences, that it can seem very strange to say that all of this has happened according to God's plan from before the creation of the world. Even an atheist would acknowledge that the belief that God is in control can be a great comfort to someone sinking in a sea of troubles. His problem is that he just does not believe it, so it offers him no comfort. He just sees the apparent tension. And he sees it as a contradiction of simple logic. If God exists and is in control, then why bother about anything?

Eternity in people's hearts (3:10-11)

Well, says the Preacher, let's talk about the human condition. He returns to the thought of 1:13, where he spoke of the burden God had placed upon man, and explains further. He agrees that man has a burden. It is not just that he needs to know about his world and has an insatiable appetite for largely futile study (1:13-18). No! He has an even deeper need. He needs to know *why* his toil — indeed, his whole life — can be of some profit in a world beyond his personal control. The

problem for the under-the-sun generation is that the idea that there is a God who orders all their 'times' and 'seasons' is a more perturbing threat to their self-image as the New Age autonomous humanity than the concept that they are alone in a dying universe. Against such practical atheism, the Preacher offers three answers.

1. Everything is beautiful (3:11)

God 'has made everything beautiful in its time' (3:11). Why go on in self-destructive scepticism? 'Care and toil begin, when faith and prayer cease; but out of care and toil we rise again to faith and prayer.'[1] The eye of faith sees the beauty in God's ordering of the times. The key to this perception is in the redemptive purposes of God for his people. All those aspects of life for which there is a time are seen in relation to the glory of the God who is saving his world, a millimetre at a time, from the institutionalized meaninglessness of satanic delusion and human emptiness. The believing church sees the heavenly symmetry of God's mighty acts in history, though invariably through the retrospective illumination of the Spirit and the Word in the arena of his faithful reflection on the signs of the times. For every believer, the gracious purposes of the Lord shine through the darkest passages of these times and, far from being a source of gloom, these become a fount of encouragement and joy in the Lord. There is a grand design. The evidence is there. Look up and see!

2. Eternity within (3:11)

God 'also ... has put eternity in [our] hearts'. Being aware of our creaturehood carries with it a sense of the reality of the Creator (Rom. 1:20; cf. Ps. 90:1-5; Eccles. 12:7). This is the basis of the ache that men and women feel for something more enduring than this life. Our hearts, said Augustine, are restless till they find their rest in the Lord.[2] The suppression of this consciousness of God is at the core of sin and estrangement from God.

3. This unfathomable life (3:11)

We cannot 'find out the work that God does from beginning to end'. Even though there is an awareness of eternity in our hearts, we cannot fully grasp its meaning. Indeed, we even *resist* the pull of eternal and spiritual matters. We look in the opposite direction for satisfaction. We imagine that secular knowledge and carnal pleasure will answer our deepest needs. And it is here that the burden is felt most painfully. The problem of 'meaning' has its only answer in heaven, from the mouth of God. But lost humanity leaves no stone unturned under the sun! We look for answers in the wrong places. How desperately we need to be found by the one whom we do not seek (Isa. 65:1)!

The gifts of God (3:12-15)

Overarching the human condition, however, is God's gracious provision (3:12-15). Quiet passion suffuses the Preacher's words. With two 'I

THINK ABOUT IT

God's will and your job

R. C. Sproul has written, 'Sometimes we fall into the trap of thinking that work is a punishment that God gave us as a result of Adam's fall in the Garden of Eden. We must remember that work was given *before* the Fall. To be sure, our labour has added burdens attached to it...[and] is accomplished by the sweat of our brow. These were the penalties of sinfulness (Gen. 3:17-19), but work itself was part of the glorious privilege granted to men and women in creation. It is impossible to understand our own humanity without understanding the central importance of work.' He goes on to point out that the Christian 'is responsible to make a contribution to the kingdom of God, to fulfil a divine mandate, to embark upon a holy calling as a servant of the living God [and] ... is keenly aware of the question, "How can I best serve God with my labour?"'*The apostle Paul tells us, 'And whatever you do in word or deed, do all in the name of the Lord Jesus, giving thanks to God the Father through Him' (Col. 3:17). Contrast this with the TGIF ('Thank God it's Friday) attitude to work so prevalent in today's so-called post-Christian culture.

*R. C. Sproul, *God's Will and the Christian* (London: Scripture Union, 1984), p. 56.

know...' statements, he affirms his most deeply held conclusions.

1. Life is from God (3:12-13)

Life is both a privilege and a pleasure for the friends of God. Complaining that God's sovereign control over everything renders our efforts meaningless is actually a veiled rationalization of practical atheism. The real argument behind such objections is this: I believe I am free and autonomous and cannot see that there is any predestinating power in control of my actions. The Preacher's point is that anyone who truly believes and trusts in God will joyfully embrace the assurance that God is in charge of the times and seasons and on that basis will gladly and gratefully receive the gifts of his loving and bountiful provision for his believing people. The children of God exult in the Lord who has cattle on a thousand hills and who is the sovereign of the created universe (Ps. 50:10; 24:1). The pursuit of God-centred and God-honouring happiness, enjoyment of good food and drink, a zeal for doing good to all men, and satisfaction in one's work — all these are legitimate goals for God's people. They are his gifts. And therefore they are our calling. The Christian is not called to live out life as a subsistence survivalist in a Kafkaesque nightmare of a world. He is called, even in the 'valley of the shadow of death' (which this world always will be until the Lord returns), to enjoy a plentiful table and the goodness and love of his Lord all the days of his life (Ps. 23:5-6).

2. Our true security (3:14-15)

The works of God endure 'forever' (3:14). They are complete and we can neither add to, nor subtract from, their ultimate perfection. Seeing how awesome his works are, 'men should fear before him' (3:14). The practical fruit of God's sovereignty will be a worshipping people, exulting in the security of their Saviour-God. And where some have to pass through the waters of persecution, there is the assurance that 'God requires an account of what is past' (3:15). The everlasting arms surround the people of God wherever they may be (Ps. 139).

The tests of life (3:16-22)

If bad experiences are sometimes blessings in disguise, they certainly can be very well disguised! Injustice and oppression scream out for redress and always persist much longer than human patience considers acceptable. There is, in our impatience, an implicit outrage against the tardiness of God to exercise what we regard as being his proper justice. It does not come naturally to us to consider that maybe, just maybe, some of the disasters and injustices were subserving the righteous purposes of God. The truth is, however, that we all want heaven now and as cheaply as possible, so we find it difficult to take the long view. Real faith is required for anyone to be willing and able to 'rest in the Lord and wait patiently for him', accepting humbly that he is truthful when he says he is 'not slack concerning his promise, as some count slackness' (Ps. 37:7; 2 Peter 3:9; cf. vv. 8-13). And the reality, or otherwise, of that faith is tested by the rampant evil that some people inflict on others.

The Preacher saw the tragedy of oppression in his own time. The doctrine of the witches in Shakespeare's *Macbeth* was stamped on the portals of Israel's justice: 'Fair is foul and foul is fair.' 'In the place of judgement, wickedness was there' (3:16). When the law becomes lawless, hope vanishes like morning dew, and moral anarchy becomes the currency of daily life in what has become no better than a dog-eat-dog world, where the biggest dog is the State! 'Where is God when we need him?' is the harsh but compelling cry of desperate pragmatism.

A twofold answer slices through the self-serving complaint that God is not fair to let such things go on.

1. Judgement ahead! (3:17)

'God shall judge the righteous and the wicked.' We are neither automata, nor are we autonomous. God gave man a certain freedom to live his life and called him to personal faith and discipleship. The Word was revealed as the rule of faith and practice. But man was not a puppet. He was called to choose whom he would serve. His response, from Adam to the present, has been to assert his autonomy from God. Well, says the Preacher,

that response was allowed for a while. As a result, the world is full of evil. The time will come for reckoning. It is appointed to man to die once and then to face judgement. There is a time for ultimate divine justice!

2. Testing now! (3:18-22)

The course of life and history is an arena of testing. 'Concerning the condition of the sons of men, God tests them, that they may see that they themselves are like animals' (3:18ff.). It is fashionable today to portray man as no more than a highly evolved animal — Desmond Morris's famous 'naked ape'. The Preacher's intention is to press the opposite point of view by showing that when man lives an under-the-sun, anti-God, anti-faith existence, he consigns himself by his own standards to a status and destiny no more significant than that of animals. They both die ... and that is *it*. By that standard, who knows where the spirits of men and animals go (3:19-21)?

The Preacher is not saying that a person who denies that he is made in the image of God and who insists on a secular earthbound lifestyle *is* no better than an animal. He is saying that his under-the-sun faith inevitably defines his existence and destiny as no different in principle from that of the animals. All we could say for sure is that, like them, we die and return to dust. Man, 'though in honour, does not remain; he is like the beasts that perish' (Ps. 49:12). But is this the last word? No, says the psalmist, 'This is the way of those who are foolish, and of their posterity who approve their sayings… But God will redeem my soul from the power of the grave; for he shall receive me' (Ps. 49:13,15).

From the perspective of a person's world view, the difference is this: As all animals are radical existentialists in that they live entirely for moment-by-moment survival and have no future beyond the expiration of life, so under-the-sun human beings turn their backs on their true nature as God's offspring, made to be his image-bearers in the world, and commit themselves to merely living for and experiencing the world in which he lives.

What waste! What eternal dereliction! What sad blasphemy! What unspeakable folly! To reject the eternal love of the Father-God! To deny the high calling of man to be the image of God and to enter into glory through a salvation bought with the blood of the incarnate Son of God! To choose meaninglessness against the destiny of fellowship with God! O, take the way of life and meaning, pleads the Preacher. Receive the gift of God!

Therefore, 'nothing is better than that a man should rejoice in his own works, for that is his heritage' (3:22). You are 'not the master of the future: therefore … rejoice in the present'.[3] God has given the present to be enjoyed as it affords God-honouring opportunities so to do. The future must be the subject of a rising personal trust in the Lord, who is ordering our lives and calling us to be his men and women in the midst of a world that so profoundly needs his saving grace.

DISCUSS IT

QUESTIONS FOR DISCUSSION

1. Even if we believe that God orders our lives, what do we still sometimes feel about life (vv. 9-10)?

2. In response to this impression, how would the Preacher answer the following questions:
   a. What is the true nature of things (v. 11)?
   b. What is the true nature of man?
   c. Why do we get confused?
   What does this tell us about our attitude to life?

3. How are we to view life (vv. 12-15)? See Psalms 24:1 and 50:10 for the basis of this outlook. How does Psalm 23:56 picture the life of God's people?

4. If life is God's gift, why can it be so hard? Why does God let such bad things go on and on? And what will he do (vv. 16-21)?

5. What does 2 Peter 3:8-13 tell us about how we respond to life (see 3:22)?

CHAPTER SEVEN

EMPTY LIVES

LOOK IT UP

BIBLE READING

Ecclesiastes 4:1-3

INTRODUCTION

Growing up in wet and windy Scotland, we always looked forward to one of those oh-so-rare 'heat waves' when a stationary ridge of high pressure would sit long enough over the country to send the temperature 'soaring' into the mid-seventies and allow us to plan rain-free picnics at the beach. Alas, every silver lining seemed to have its cloud! During these still periods, the mornings would often be enveloped by the 'haar' — a cold, clinging mist that even in mid-July can chill you to the bone! The best of things can so easily be blighted by an unexpected turn. Disappointment can come like that summer mist and make the best projects seem utterly pointless.

The clammy tentacles of emptiness insinuate themselves into the happiest of lives and create a hollow feeling that can crush the spirit and bring a gnawing despair. The Preacher turns to a problem that threatens the most normal and tranquil of lives — the emptiness of earthly values in the context of particular, perennial and potentially threatening social problems. He begins here to expound his main argument.

The scope of the problem

In the first three chapters, he sets the scene by survey-ing the general contours of our human predicament and the associated issues with which we must grapple in order to make sense and success of our lives. He spoke of the spiritual bankruptcy of secular, under-the-sun living (1:1 - 2:23). By way of contrast, he pointed briefly to the alternative, the life of faith in God (2:24-26). Finally, he argued for the certainties of God's provi-dence and final judgement, urging, by implication, the necessity of receiving and enjoying life as the gift of God (3:1-22).

The next seven chapters (4:1 - 10:20) flesh out this thesis by highlighting particular problems and pointing to the Lord's answers. The recurring twin themes are, on the one hand, the utter emptiness of worldly values and, on the other hand, the meaning and joy that is to be found exclusively in a living faith relationship to God.

The 'rat race'

Ecclesiastes 4 isolates the practical problem of what we today might call 'the rat race'. Every generation tends, in its superior, self-centred way, to think of its own situation as unique. And, of course, it is true that each age has its own character with new problems calling for fresh answers. We do not readily think of first millennium B.C. society as fitting the image conjured up by the term 'rat race'. Nevertheless, there were indeed analogous, if not exactly identical, pressures on the people of those distant centuries. When we filter out the hard core of their problems from their specific manifestation in the context of that day, we find that they touch our own lives in a very close and affecting way. The Preacher takes the widest view of this phenomenon, touching upon major representative features that combine to erode the meaningfulness of people's lives. He begins with some grim observations about oppression and injustice, especially with reference to its devastating effect on those who suffer its depredations (4:1-3), and he ends with a sombre assessment of the position of those most likely perpetrators of oppression — kings, who for all their power and fame, often live lonely lives, after which their memory recedes into an execrated past (4:13-16).

The tears of the oppressed (4:1)

'A sinful world', said Charles Bridges, 'is a world of selfishness.'[1] The world is full of oppressive governments, exploitative businesses and, not least, people who simply take advantage of others. The Robin Hood type of legend is so powerfully appealing precisely because of the generally oppressive climate of human societies. For many, if not most, people from the past to the present, freedom extends little further than the door of the soul. The Swiss-based organization, Christian Solidarity International — a society that is committed to supporting Christians under persecution from the State throughout the world with a ministry of prayer, public awareness and legal representation — not long ago listed over fifty countries where governments harass, proscribe or persecute faithful Christian witness.[2] In the democratic West, the inundation of the courts with lawsuits and criminal prosecutions; the overcrowding of the prisons; and, most poignantly, the roll of abused children, rape victims, the swindled, the maimed, and the murdered all cry to heaven for justice on behalf of the prey of the oppressors.

God condemns such oppression in his Word in the strongest and most comprehensive terms. The Scriptures roundly condemn all exploitation, whether by the state (Prov. 28:16), the wealthy (Amos 4:1), the law (Amos 5:12), the church (1 Sam. 2:12-17; Matt. 23:23-24; cf. 1 Peter 5:1-5), employers (Deut. 24:14), property agents (Mic. 2:2), bankers (Ezek. 22:12,29), or businessmen (Hos. 12:7). And yet, there is so little concern for those who are lashed by the waves of cynical plundering. The Preacher cries, 'And look! The tears of the oppressed, but they have no comforter; on the side of their oppressors there is power, but they have no comforter' (4:1).

Abortion and the 'culture of death'

Charles Colson describes Western society as embracing 'a culture of death'.* He has noted that, in the USA, 'The first public official to declare abortion a positive health policy was Arkansas State Health Director Joycelyn Elders, later surgeon general of the United States [in the Clinton administration]. Abortion, she said, has "an important and positive public health effect", reducing, "the number of children afflicted with severe defects". Abortion was no longer treated as a wrenching tragedy, a decision reached with agonizing reluctance. Instead, it was a positive good — a means for improving the species' (p. 121). The butchering of the unborn has become a moral good and an evolutionary tool to advance humanity!

Colson also notes that 'once the principle of autonomy and choice [i.e., freedom from accountability to God and the standard of divine law] is established, there is no way to maintain a higher value for life' (p. 123). Why? Because *my* standard is what suits me, and, without any absolute ethical restraints, I will act in my own interest, sometimes very selfishly. 'The supremely tragic irony in all of this is that a supposedly exalted view of human reason has led to such a degraded view of human life. When Descartes declared, "I think, therefore I am," he had no idea his slogan would lead to a culture in which what I am is determined by what *other* people think' (p. 126).

* C. Colson, *How now shall we live?* (Wheaton, Illinois: Tyndale, 1999).

The psalmist pleaded, 'Look on my right hand and see; for there is no one acknowledges me; refuge has failed me; no one cares for my soul' (Ps. 142:4). The dying in the streets of Calcutta or the destitute in the barrios (districts) of Latin America might say the same today. This is the universal cry of the oppressed.

The ultimate experience of oppression was, of course, that of the Lord Jesus Christ himself. He was hated in spite of his perfect sinlessness — or, rather, precisely because of it. Speaking of this hatred, he said, 'But this is to fulfil what is written in their Law: "They hated me without reason"' (John 15:25, NIV). The words quoted by the Lord are from Psalm 69:4, a passage that describes prophetically the experience of Christ at the hands of his detractors. 'Scorn has broken my heart and has left me helpless; I looked for sympathy, but there was none, for comforters, but I found none' (Ps. 69:20, NIV).

The Christian response to the cry of the oppressed is supposed to be precisely the opposite of this sort of treatment. We are, for example, to 'remember those in prison as if [we] were their fellow prisoners' (Heb. 13:3, NIV). This flows from the central truth of the gospel, namely, that Jesus subjected himself to humiliation and suffering, including not only the unjust oppression of wicked men, but also the wholly just wrath of God against *our* sins. He did this to redeem us from sin by making atonement as the substitute who bears that sin in the place of sinners—taking and satisfying the penalty due to them. Part of that great complex of sin is a disturbing lack of compassion. In the parable of the

good Samaritan, Jesus vividly highlighted the callous indifference of the Levite, who when he spotted the victim of the Jericho Road muggers, preferred to pass by on the other side, not to get involved, and, needless to say, leave the compassion to somebody else — in that case to a despised (by Jews) Samaritan! Jesus' sufferings and death were the supreme act of compassion. He was despised and rejected by men, a man of sorrows and familiar with suffering. But when we hid, as it were, our faces from him (Isa. 53:3), he answered our hard hearts with steadfast love and sovereignly given and freely bestowed grace (Rom. 5:6). For this reason, the first evidence of having truly received Christ — the first fruit of the Holy Spirit's work of grace in our hearts — is a love for the Lord that overflows with compassion for others in their need. In the New Testament era, which means *right now,* some oppressed soul should be able to say, 'I looked for sympathy ... and I found Christ ... in the compassionate love of his people!' Where there are Christians, compassion should flow like a mighty river.

Grateful dead and happy never-borns (4:2-3)

A world full of oppression, assessed in purely secular terms, offers little or no hope of any redressing of the imbalances of injustice and lack of compassion. It presents a depressing canvas of unrelieved and largely irretrievable injustice and misery. And this may be said in spite of all the institutionalized compassion of secular society through wealth redistribution and social engineering programmes. There is even evidence, as Herbert Schlossberg puts it, that 'the source of the problem is in its putative solution';[3] that is to say, these expressions of the secular 'caring society' have been counterproductive and have actually exacerbated the problems they were designed to relieve. Be that as it may, it is small wonder in the face of present realities that thoughts of death as the great escape route begin to spring up in the minds of an increasing number of people.

The Preacher anticipates this — and even goes beyond it — in what has to be one of the most brutally frank expositions of the naked emptiness of the 'hope' of the godless secularist. The dead are better off than the living, he says, but the unborn are better off than both, for they have 'not seen the evil work that is done under the sun' (4:2-3).

Here is one of the arguments for abortion in our day — better no life at all than the misery of an 'unwanted' one. We rightly identify this as a culture of death masquerading as moral high ground. It is small wonder that the so-called 'post-Christian' twentieth century ushered in an age of death by wars, gas-ovens and abortionist scalpels and syringes. The hopelessness outlined by Solomon three millennia ago now has the tools to express itself in the mass self-destruction of godless human societies!

DISCUSS IT

Let us not miss the message in this contemporary carnage. What the Preacher's astonishingly provocative statement as good as says is that the only good secular humanist is not even a dead one, but one who has never existed! He is saying that from God's point of view that is as much hope and as much meaning as an under-the-sun life can provide. But empty lives and the tears of the oppressed surely cry out for something better.

QUESTIONS FOR DISCUSSION

1. What is God's attitude to oppression (4:1)?

2. What did Jesus experience (John 15:25), and what ought to be the Christian's response (Heb. 13:3; Luke 10:25-37)?

3. In what sense does Solomon suggest the dead may be better off than the living (4:2)? Is this what he really believes?

4. Discuss the burden of existence devoid of purpose and hope (4:3). What is the solution?

CHAPTER EIGHT

THE
RAT RACE

BIBLE READING

Ecclesiastes 4:4-16

In the opening section of the chapter (4:1-3) Solomon reflects on the 'oppression that is done under the sun'. The victims are powerless. So if that is all there is 'under the sun', then you might argue that the dead and the never-born are better off. It is a stark picture of the futility of a closed-system 'under-the-sun' world.

Although he never mentions it, Solomon's implication is that a large proportion of human achievement is gained at the expense of the oppressed. He therefore turns to the thought that envy is the engine of much of what is usually regarded as success. He challenges us about the attitudes we bring to work and achievement. Is the world of work just a 'rat race'? Or is there a meaningful end in view? He covers three subjects that in their own ways tend to define the way people think of success. The first is the business of making money (4:4-6), the second is the desire to leave a lasting legacy (4:7-12) and the third is exercising power and influence (4:13-16).

Making money (4:4-6)

With vivid simplicity, the alternatives are sketched in terms of three sets of hands and how they are used — or not used, as the case may be — in the pursuit of a happy and productive life.

1. Two hands working away (4:6)

'Both hands full, together with toil' symbolizes the grasping obsession with ever-growing affluence. The corporate raider restlessly scans the stock market for new acquisitions for his business empire; the 'workaholic' slaves compulsively for his first million ... and his second, too. The 'yuppies' (young upwardly mobile professionals) manoeuvre themselves with calculated deftness toward the apex of the corporate ladders of our time. The common factor is an impenetrable preoccupation with personal advancement. What we *want*, we define in terms of need, and since it is inevitable that what we believe we need must be good, our personal goals, thus qualified, become the driving imperatives of life. Ambition becomes necessity; necessity becomes a god. In his penetrating study of the modern concept of need, Tony Walter shows how the abandonment of moral and spiritual obligation to God has led to the widespread assumption that 'the individual himself or herself, and his closest loved ones, are seen as a person's ultimate frame of reference'. Consequently, 'meeting the needs of the self is increasingly

talked of as life's project'.¹ 'Need is the religion of the religionless, the morality of those who pride themselves on having progressed beyond morality.'² This is just the contemporary face of the Preacher's 'both hands full ... with toil'. Both hands are into possessions. That person is totally committed to the world's standard for success, and he is driven by the envy of his neighbour (4:4).

2. Two hands folded in inactivity (4:5)

Folded hands symbolize the position of the drop-out. 'The fool folds his hands and consumes his own flesh' (4:5; Prov. 6:10). This is the opposite extreme from the rat race. He ruins himself — literally, eats his own flesh (which is what you do if you don't eat). His is a cannibalism of the whole man, body and soul. His life at least has the advantage of being quiet — of a kind — but it is essentially self-destructive. And God's Word is clear that a man who 'will not work, neither shall he eat' (2 Thess. 3:10), while he who refuses to provide for his own family 'has denied the faith and is worse than an unbeliever' (1 Tim. 5:8). Strong words these, but no less dire than the consequences of indolence in the lives of the dropouts and their dependants. Escapism may feel good at the time, but it is no solution. The escapist has jumped from the frying pan into the fire.

3. One hand working (4:6)

There is another way. 'Better a handful with quietness' (4:6). This beautiful expression is presented as a middle way between two-fisted grasping and hand-folding laziness. But it is far more than a balance between two extremes — it is a radical alternative to two essentially sinful positions. The idea is of a modest and contented life, in which one hand is put forth effectively and successfully but garners tranquillity in the process. It is possible to have genuine peace *and* the prosperity with which God would reward our labours. But what is the other hand doing? The Bible says that the basic fact of the life of the Lord's disciples is that they are always with their Lord, who holds them by their 'right hand' (Ps. 73:23). The condition of a happy balance in life is that the right hand — signifying our primary motive — is in the hand of our Father-God, while the left hand is put forth in fruitful and satisfying labour in commitment to the revealed purposes of God. The children's hymn by Henry E. Button is near to the mark, in spite of its overtones of middle-class sentimentalism:

O what can little hands do
    To please the King of Heaven?
The little hands some work may try,
To help the poor in misery:
    Such grace to mine be given.

In terms of the fulness of Jesus Christ, we are called to life in him — to 'treasures in heaven' (Matt. 6:19-21),

THINK ABOUT IT

Having a 'calling'

1 Corinthians 7:20f. tells us that newly-converted Christians are to 'remain in the same calling [i.e., job] in which he was called [i.e. became a Christian]'. Paul Helm points out that this is 'of fundamental importance for an understanding of the Christian's relationship to daily life... So a Christian has two callings. He is effectually called by grace, converted. In addition there is a call of a different kind, that which is provided by the network of circumstance, personal relations, past history, in which he is found when God's grace comes to him.'* This obviously does not apply to inherently sinful activities, like being a Mafia hit-man or a prostitute. Positively, it implies that our work is to be seen as a calling before God. You are not to look for a new calling just because you became a Christian.

This also challenges the common assumption in our world that work is just a necessary evil. 'TGIF' (Thank God it's Friday) is the cry of a generation that worships leisure and sees no 'calling' in labour. How do you view your various circumstances in life — whether your job, your personal abilities (or disabilities), an infirm parent requiring care, and the like? Are these just curses to you? How do you tackle such challenges? Or do you walk away?

* P. Helm, *The Callings. The Gospel in the World* (Edinburgh: Banner of Truth, 1987), p. 48.

to serving God, not riches (Matt. 6:24), and to depend upon his provision for our every need (Matt. 6:25-34). Therefore, 'whatever you do, do it heartily, as to the Lord and not to men' (Col. 3:23). Every other approach is 'grasping for the wind' (4:6)!

An enduring legacy (4:7-12)

Successful people are often lonely in the crowd. Ebenezer Scrooge, in Charles Dickens' *A Christmas Carol,* was a sad and lonely man until Tiny Tim melted his miserly soul. Billionaire Howard Hughes ended his days a chronic recluse, haunted by his fears of disease — a living-death testimony to the impotence (or was it the danger?) of material prosperity in the face of profound spiritual darkness. Isolation is often the companion of worldly success. The amiable chatter at celebrity cocktail parties may only mask aching oceans of loneliness. Indeed, being in the presence of so much superficial conviviality only serves to underline the emptiness of such relationships, at least for those who long for genuine companionship. Another aspect of this loneliness is the fear of leaving no lasting legacy — that this success will have no successor.

1. A man alone (4:7-8)

The Preacher brings these twin themes together — success and loneliness — in reference to a man who had

no family to whom he could give support in his lifetime and leave his money after his death. He was torn between his overwhelming lust for greater wealth and the obvious senselessness of doing all this when he had no children of his own. He had good reason to ask the question, 'For whom do I toil?' (4:8). Avarice is always a hard, and less than rational, taskmaster! This man was a slave to moneymaking: it was a case of 'the less need, the more raking'.[3] And to the extent he was enslaved, he was, as Derek Kidner trenchantly observes, 'virtually dehumanized, for he [had] surrendered to a mere craving and to the endless process of feeding it'.[4] This is more obviously meaningless in view of his lack of dependants or heirs, but many children have had a father like him, and many a wife such a husband. They never saw him from one day's end to another, and when their paths did cross, it was as ships passing in the night. The Preacher's workaholic at least had no family to neglect! His latter-day descendants will be buried in their work on the day when Christ returns to judge the living and the dead. This is what the worship of self can do to us!

2. Two are better than one (4:9-12)

It is as well to remember that the Preacher was speaking to the people of God. Yes! It is very possible for Christians to throw themselves into dysfunctional patterns of life. Devoted pastors have sacrificed their families on the altar of an exaggerated and unbalanced view of their calling. Christian businessmen can enjoy making money and find it a deal easier than the work of forging a healthy home life in loving and patient co-operation with wife and children. Some men live like bachelors all their married lives, to the eternal frustration of their wives and families. Not being alone means far more than merely having people that you can call loved ones or friends. The antidote to loneliness is practical companionship and the principle, as stated by the Preacher, is that 'two are better than one, because they have a good reward for their labour' (4:9). In a real partnership, the whole is better than the sum of its parts: for, if two are better than one, they are also better than both of the ones, when they are alone!

The practical blessings of companionship are probably too numerous to detail, so Solomon contents himself with a few leading examples.

a. Friendship (4:9-10). A friend in need — your need, not his — is a friend indeed. 'Woe to him who is alone when he falls, for he has no one to help him up' (4:10). If you have had either experience, you know the force of the Preacher's point. I learned something of this one bitter January in a rowing boat on the River Ythan in Aberdeenshire, in Scotland. I was taking core samples of estuarine mud for my research on a worm called

Scoloplos armiger. As I sifted through one sample, the intense cold froze my hands and I fainted away, apparently in shock. When I came to, my friend Dick Marriott (who was looking for eider duck regurgitations in the same mud flat) was straightening me out in the bottom of the boat. I recall two things from that point until we got to the shore. One was his typically English understatement, when, with a chuckle he said, 'Just as well you didn't fall out of the boat, old boy — I'd have had to row away without you!' The other was how thankful to God I was for such a friend, for that was the one thing he would never have done.

b. Coziness (4:11). 'If two lie down together, they will keep warm' (4:11). This is often taken to refer to a husband and wife, but it has, in fact, a wider reference. In days gone by, travellers used to bundle up close together at night for warmth. In the guardhouse at Old Fort Niagara, New York, you can see a bed on which twelve soldiers could sleep in their uniforms to keep warm and be ready for action if awakened by the sentries.

c. Security (4:12). Companions provide collective security. 'Though one may be overpowered by another, two can withstand him' (4:12). The man who fell among thieves on the road to Jericho was alone. There is some strength in numbers.

d. Strength (4:12). The ties that bind also give strength.
'A threefold cord is not quickly broken' (4:12). The pre-
vious illustrations focus on the advantages of two over
one. Here a standard cord of three strands suggests that
three will be even better than two. In New Testament
terms we are reminded of the two on the road to
Emmaus who were joined by a third, 'the risen Christ',
and could later testify how their hearts had burned
within them as the Lord fellowshipped with them along
the road (Luke 24:32). Jesus sent his disciples out in
twos (Matt. 10:1-6), but it is always his presence as the
invisible third companion that is the power lending
wings to their witness (Matt. 28:18-20). The close
intertwining of the three cords also suggests that it is
not numbers *per se*, but the quality of the binding ties
of fellowship that are of critical significance. Quality
as opposed to quantity, and personal commitment
rather than mere strength in numbers, are what make
this companionship a profound blessing for those who
enjoy it. Believers are 'heirs *together* of the grace of life'
(1 Peter 3:7). It is *in Christ* that *we* (together) shall be
more than conquerors (Rom. 8:37). The sharing of our
lives with one another flows from the one salvation in
Christ our Saviour (Acts 2:42; 2 Cor. 8:5). This rebukes
the religious loner, 'who belongs to no Church, because
no Church is perfect enough for him',[5] and calls us to a
practical membership one with another. As with all the
Preacher's solutions to human problems, the answer
leads ultimately to a life of faith in the Lord. Without
that, life is truly an empty existence.

Power and influence (4:13-16)

If money cannot insulate someone against loneliness, how about power and position? The
answer is so obvious that it might be more intelligent to ask why anybody would want to be a
king or a president! Rulers soon find that the
higher up a mountain you climb, the colder it
gets. And how much less room there is at the
top. The corridors of power are lonely places.
Today's hero is tomorrow's pariah. The comforts
of a good showing in the polls are fleeting at best.

The Preacher tells the story of 'an old but foolish king' who was supplanted by 'a poor but wise
youth', only to find that the latter also eventually fell out of favour with his former support-
ers. He suffers what Herbert Leupold calls 'the
common fate of rulers'.[6] Even in the relative tranquillity of the Western democracies, where
elections rather than military coups change the
governments, political longevity is at the mercy
of an electorate with an attention span of a television commercial. And landslide election victories are aptly named — because real landslides
are caused by shifting, unstable earth! This
points to the vanity of thinking that political
power or public acclaim will in itself somehow
rise above the transience and meaninglessness
of life lived under the sun. The few who are put
into the position where, in theory, they should

be able to implement their 'If-I-were-king' ambitions find that they have reached 'a pinnacle of human glory, only to be stranded there'.⁷ Mr Pickwick might well sing (in the musical version of *The Pickwick Papers*), 'If I ruled the world, every day would be the first day of spring,' but the real world is something else.

What is Solomon saying? Simply that meaningless-ness is inevitable in a life lived in terms of under-the-sun secularism. Oppression continues year after year, even human achievement owes more to envy than to altruism, and, in any case, wealth and power *per se* seem to exacerbate rather than ameliorate the empti-ness that so many people feel. Although not stated by the Preacher, the answer is to be found only in the liv-ing God and in the Lordship of the Son who was yet to be revealed in the fulness of time. No one can read Ecclesiastes 4 without being driven back to chapter 3 — to the conclusion that 'every man should eat and drink and enjoy the good of all his labour — it is the gift of God' (3:13). To receive the gift, however, we must receive the Giver. And that is the rub for secular under-the-sun men and women! The power and influence that secures the meaning in our life is that of the God and Father of the Lord Jesus Christ.

What does worldly influence count against the as-surance of the love of God in the incarnate Christ, the promise of salvation from sin through the crucified Christ, and the prospect of perfect fellowship with God with the exalted Christ? Such living hope 'is built on nothing less than Jesus' blood and righteousness'.

QUESTIONS FOR DISCUSSION

DISCUSS IT

1. Why is 'a handful with quietness' (4:6) to be preferred to two full hands (4:6) and folded hands (4:5; see Prov. 6:10; 2 Thess. 3:10; 1 Tim. 5:8)?

2. What four examples prove that two (or three) are better than one (4:9-12)?

3. What insights can you glean from Luke 24:32; Matthew 10:16 and 28:18-20; and 1 Peter 3:7?

4. What is the lesson of the foolish king and the wise youth? Look back to 3:13.

CHAPTER NINE

HOLLOW
RELIGION

BIBLE READING

Ecclesiastes 5:1-3

In the popular mind, 'religion' is an ugly word. 'Religion' is, by and large, what other people 'get', and 'religious' is what other people are. Agnostics and evangelicals, if they agree on nothing else, will unite in denying that they have a religion. At the same time, the former will claim to have no faith while the latter will cheerfully confess a supernaturalist biblical faith in Jesus Christ. For the sceptics, all faith is religion and to be rejected as a mystical hoax. For Christian believers, faith is belief of the truth and a good thing, while religion is equated with nominal and outward formalism and is therefore a bad thing.

This distinction goes back a long way. For example, the eighteenth-century poet, Robert Burns, uses it to contrast the simple fervent faith of a Scottish cottager (thought to be his father) with the showy religiosity of the Establishment. Having described family worship as it was and still is practised among godly Presbyterian folk in Scotland — the singing of a psalm, reading of Scripture, and kneeling for extempore prayer — he writes:

> Compar'd with this, how poor Religion's pride,
>   In all the pomp of method, and of art;
> When men display to congregations wide
>   Devotion's ev'ry grace, except the heart!
> The Power, incens'd, the pageant will desert,
> The pompous strain, the sacerdotal stole:
>   But haply, in some cottage far apart,
> May hear, well pleas'd, the language of the soul,
> And in His Book of Life the inmates poor enroll.[1]

Burns was an Enlightenment man, and therefore a sceptic in matters of religion, but it must be admitted that he has a very valid point about 'Religion's pride'. There is a self-evident hollowness in much of what passes for Christianity in this world of ours. And as it was a stumbling block for Robert Burns two centuries ago, so it is today for millions of people within and without the borders of institutional Christianity.

How *not* to approach God

How is God to be approached? How are we to worship and serve him? Where does God fit in the human experience? And what use is all the religion in this world, when it seems as if it is all going to hell on a roller coaster? If God is supposed to be the solution to our

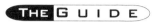

deepest problems, why is there so much religion and precious little real faith?

Solomon has been concerned to show the meaninglessness of life lived under the sun — that is, without reference to God as the ultimate reality. In the course of this discussion he hints at the answer to the problem. There is the potential for joy and satisfaction, and it is in pleasing God (2:24-26). There is also the fact that God rules all of history and will judge in perfect righteousness (3:1-22). Yes, says the Preacher, there is meaning in life, but it is only going to be found in a faith relationship to the Lord. Only in him can we understand correctly this world in which he has placed us. And only in him can we cope with the challenges it presents. When we relate this to the emptiness of human lives and, specifically, the soul-destroying loneliness that so many people feel (4:1-16), we must see that the answer is to know the Lord personally as 'a friend who sticks closer than a brother' (Prov. 18:24). He is the missing companion. He is the giver of life and of ultimate meaningfulness.

But the Preacher is aware of the fact that religion and man's approach to God can be corrupted along with everything else in a sin-sick world. So how do his gentle pointers to an answer that says, 'Meaning will be found in true faith in God,' mesh with the abounding evidence that so much religion seems little better than a charade and looks pretty meaningless itself? Is religion not also 'a grasping for the wind'? The Preacher knows how easy it is for us to go through the motions, whether it is telling beads or singing hymns. He wants us to distinguish an empty, meaningless religion from the real thing. He wants us to root out formalism and come to experience living communion with the Lord. Consequently, he begins with that most fundamental element of Christian experience — the worshippers' approach to God.

How to approach God

We could no doubt argue for ever about theological positions and which denominations have the most biblical practice of worship. We could discuss, as has Herbert Schlossberg so brilliantly, the ways in which the church has set aside God's Word in favour of embracing, promoting, and even idolizing the spirit of the age and the cultural norms or secular (i.e. under-the-sun) society.[2] But the Preacher begins with your first step toward God. And he knows that no one can hide from such a question. After all, we all have a real, definable experience (or non-experience) of worshipping God. We know, each and every one of us, who we think God is, and we know well the attitudes we bring to our approach to him. Of course, the Preacher is speaking primarily to the professed people of God. His point of contact is their actual piety, such as it might be. And

True prayer or whistling in the dark?

Indistinct views of God make for indistinct views of prayer. Many seem to believe there is some kind of a 'God' out there, but have no conviction that he is the God and Father of the Lord Jesus Christ. Someone once quipped that prayer to such a vague impersonal deity should begin, 'To whom it may concern...' Such prayer is like sending radio messages into space on the off-chance someone might be out there to pick them up.

While in prison in Bedford in 1662, John Bunyan wrote a wonderful little book on prayer, entitled in the style of that time, *I will pray with the spirit and the understanding also*. In it, he defines true prayer as 'a sincere, sensible, affectionate pouring out of the heart or soul to God, through Christ, in the strength and assistance of the Holy Spirit, for such things as God has promised, or according to his Word, for the good of the church, with submission in faith to the will of God.'* There may be 'no atheists in foxholes' when bullets are flying, but being in a state of fear is not the same thing as coming to God, believing that he is, and is a rewarder of those who diligently seek him (Heb. 11:6). Shouting 'Help!' into the vague beyond is not the same as crying 'God be merciful to me a sinner!' (Luke 18:13). Sincere unbelief is not nearly enough. Neither is sincere false religion, or good intentions, or any other form of 'will-worship' (Col. 2:23, AV). However, if you really are at an end of your tether and you call on God by his right name and through the only mediator between you and him, Jesus Christ (1 Tim. 2:5), he will hear you and you will know it.

* John Bunyan, *Prayer* (London: Banner of Truth, 1965), p. 13.

his discussion penetrates behind the screen, as it so often is, of creedal definitions and theological shop-talk to lay the claims of God upon the conscience and demand a practical response, whether of faith or (God forbid!) unbelief. If your life seems to be meaningless, then realize that it is because meaninglessness in one form or another is lodged within your heart. Meaning-lessness cannot be imposed from outside upon a heart that has been reborn by the Holy Spirit and reformed by saving faith in Christ. But, like any other manifest-ation of rebellion against God, it can be entertained and indulged as the Christian wavers in his faithful-ness to Jesus Christ.

Central to the Christian life is the principle that our *inward* obedience is to run parallel to our *outward* obed-ience.[3] When the latter is slowly eroding, as it was in the Preacher's Israel (Neh. 13:10-20; Mal. 1:8), it is clear that hearts are no longer turned to the Lord as they ought to be. The Bible consistently addresses the ne-cessity of a careful outward conformity to God's will, built upon an inward love and devotion toward him as a personal Father-God, in Jesus Christ. From the heart to the hand, we are called to joyous discipleship. We are not to be like those who honour God with their lips, while their hearts are far from him (Mark 7:6). The Preacher, then, has a message for the person who, as Kidner so neatly puts it, 'likes a good sing and turns up cheerfully enough to church: but who listens with half an ear and never quite gets round to what he has volunteered to do for God'.[4]

WHAT THE TEXT TEACHES

1. Reverence (5:1)

We must never forget who God is. 'Walk prudently when you go to the house of God.' The text says literally, 'Watch your feet.' The same expression occurs in Isaiah 58:13, where we are encouraged to keep our feet from breaking the Sabbath. The idea is that when we are not careful to do God's will, we will inevitably trample upon it. Where we put our feet tells something about our attitude. You might say that we vote with our feet!

A related piece of symbolism is found in Moses' encounter with God at the burning bush. God instructed Moses to remove his sandals, because the ground on which he stood was holy (Exod. 3:5). Moses' feet must be clean in the presence of God — for this was the outward sign of an inward reverence for the living God.[5]

The 'house of God' refers to the worship of God, preeminently the temple in Jerusalem but perhaps also the local synagogues throughout post-exilic Judea.[6] Throughout the history of Israel, the temple was where God revealed himself to his people in a palpable manifestation of his glory. 'Holiness adorns your house,' said the psalmist. 'In reverence will I bow down toward your holy temple' (Ps. 93:5; 5:7, NIV). The recapture of a reverent approach to the worship of God is an urgent necessity in the modern church.

The attitudes we bring to worship and the way we carry ourselves as we ostensibly come into God's presence are in desperate need of reformation. The preparation of the heart in quietness before the call to worship; the holy abandonment to full-throated praise; the bated breath of expectancy in prayer, punctuated by the 'amens' of the soul, audible and/or inaudible; the sense of the Holy Spirit enveloping us in the act of worship, leading our hearts and minds to spiritual blessings in heavenly places in Christ (Eph. 1:3; 2:6); the joyous reception of the bread of life as the Word is opened; and the exultant celebration of our risen Saviour as the blessing of God in Christ is poured out according to promise. For this to be a reality, we must be willing to concentrate our minds on the things above, not on earthly things (Col. 3:2). And only a clear view of the majesty of the God we worship will draw out such gripping, exhilarating reverence. God is our Creator, our Redeemer, and our Comforter. Every moment of living worship acknowledges this truth with joy.

2. A ready ear (5:1)

We must listen to what God says. Ears come before lips in the order of Christian growth. 'Therefore take heed how you hear,' said Jesus. 'For whoever has, to him more will be given; and whoever does not have, even what he seems to have will be taken from him' (Luke 8:18). Having presupposes listening and assimilating. Yet some Christians are so full of what they are going to

share with others that there is little opportunity, or even inclination, to be quiet and hear what God is saying. 'Be still, and know that I am God' (Ps. 46:10) must call forth the response, 'I will hear what God the LORD will speak, for he will speak peace to his people and to his saints; but let them not turn back to folly' (Ps. 85:8). The caveat is appropriate, for the problem of the Israelites was that too often 'the word which they heard did not profit them, not being mixed with faith in those who heard it' (Heb. 4:2). To go into God's presence and not hear what he is saying, is, says the Preacher, 'to give the sacrifice of fools, for they do not know that they do evil' (5:1). It is irrational, if not indeed dangerous, to attend an audience with a powerful ruler and then wilfully disregard all that he says. It is God who says that the sacrifice of the wicked is an abomination (Prov. 15:8). His words are spirit and they are life (John 6:63). How we then should hang upon his every utterance and take them to heart with thanksgiving!

3. Careful words (5:2-3)

Likewise, we must guard our lips. 'God is in heaven and you on earth; therefore let your words be few' (5:2). Prayer is not to be blighted by hastiness or wordiness. Again the warning is against empty formal prayers. The Lord is not impressed by 'babbling like pagans' or multiplication of prayers (Matt. 6:7, NIV; Isa. 1:15). 'In the multitude of words, sin is not lacking' (Prov. 10:19). Unless we come to the Lord humbly, reverently and repentantly, 'prayer is lost breath'.[7] On the other hand, 'the effective, fervent prayer of a righteous man avails much' (James 5:16). The spirit of true prayer was summed up by our Lord when he said to his disciples after the Last Supper, 'If you abide in me, and *my words abide in you*, you will ask what you desire, and it shall be done for you' (John 15:7). In the face of the severest threat to the fledgling church, the apostles and the believers held a prayer meeting (Acts 4:24-31). The record of that prayer is a marvellous practical example of what the Preacher is enjoining upon us. The prayer is short. It begins with the worship and adoration of God (v. 24), continues with the application of Scripture to the precise problem facing the believers (vv. 25-28) and makes just one request (vv. 29-30). The answer follows with dramatic and powerful immediacy (v. 31).

Evangelicals are inclined to equate formalism in worship with time-honoured rubrics, from the high liturgics of Rome to the 'four walls and a sermon' of the Presbyterians. Clerical garb, pipe organs, recited prayers and programmed responses are seen as the tentacles of a cold and mechanical performance that simulates rather than expresses a lively approach to the worship of God. While there is, no doubt, some truth in this charge, it is not without the taint of a self-serving spirit. We may have escaped the ritual of the read prayers of the Prayer Book or the Pastor's Annual, but instead we find ourselves buried in a veritable landslide of prayer requests, many of them trivial and some of them verging on gossip. We don't recite prayers perhaps, but our 'spontaneous' extempore prayers can be as ritually predictable (and not nearly as beautiful or profound) as, for instance, those of the old Anglican Prayer Book. This is not so much an argument for the latter as it is a caution against dead 'spontaneity'. In the same vein, guitar accompaniment becomes received orthodoxy and repetitive mantra-like choruses are held as indicating a truly lively faith. Isn't it funny how it is always the other people who are needing to be liberated from forms and traditions? The truth is, that it is too easy to trade new ritual for old and create a different formalism, the nature of which is masked by its initial novelty and seeming radicalism. My point is not to discuss the relative merits of these methods, but to emphasize that it is from the *heart* that issues of life proceed. There are certainly rights and wrongs, proprieties and improprieties, reverences and irreverences in the way we worship God. But behind all this is the attitude of heart that gives them birth and expression. And crucial is a deep sense of who God is and our consequent felt need of his loving, merciful, gracious and joyous fellowship in Jesus Christ.

QUESTIONS FOR DISCUSSION

1. Why must we guard our steps when we worship God (5:1; see also Exod. 3:3; Isa. 58:13)?

2. Why do ears come before the tongue in the order of Christian growth (see Luke 8:18; Ps. 46:10; 85:8)?

3. Why should our words be few in our prayers (5:2-3; see also Isa. 1:15; Prov. 10:19; Matt. 6:7)?

4. Discuss Acts 4:24-31 as a model for our praying.

CHAPTER TEN

PROMISES TO KEEP

LOOK IT UP

BIBLE READING

Ecclesiastes 5:4-7

INTRODUCTION

The expression, 'Laws are made to be broken,' is surely a sad comment on human perversity. This easily extends to promises as well. It would be interesting, in a depressing kind of way, to know how many promises are made every day in this world, that are destined never to be kept. To come closer to home, we might narrow it to the undertakings that Christians make in the context of their own local church. How lightly, it seems, we say we will do something and then never do it at all. Then, to explain away our negligence, we resort to all sorts of ingenious excuses and special pleading to justify ourselves.

Of even deeper significance are the promises that people make to God and later do not keep. In the fellowship within which I minister, members are received on a profession of faith in Jesus Christ and affirm a 'Covenant of Church Membership' in which they solemnly promise to be a living part of the congregation of the Lord's people. We all promise to heed, in the Lord, the teaching and the discipline of the fellowship. We commit ourselves to Bible reading, prayer, keeping the Lord's Day, attending public worship, observing the sacraments, giving to the Lord's work, and ministering to one another and, most searchingly, to 'forsake all sin' and conform our lives to the teaching and example of the Lord.[1] These are, or should be, very normal and standard components of membership in the churches of the Protestant Reformation — so much so, that sometimes the 'I dos' and 'I wills' can roll off our tongues with too much ease. They are, nevertheless, profound commitments that are taken very seriously by the Lord and ought to so be taken by us.

Vows are to be kept (5:4)

When the Preacher spoke of vows, however, he was not thinking so much of the promises, like terms of church membership commitment, that we make to keep what God commands of us anyway. To promise to do what he has specifically told us to do is only our reasonable service to him. The Preacher had in mind voluntary vows that Old Testament believers made to God, especially in connection with the worship and sacrificial offerings of the temple, although sometimes in terms of self-denying devotional commitments, such as the Nazirite vow (Num. 6). These could take any number of forms, from Hannah's dedication of a son, to Jonah's reaffirmation of an earlier commitment to the Lord (1 Sam. 1:11; Jonah 2:9). These were spontaneous and voluntary. God always required obedience

but he did not require these specific vows. Scripture makes two clear rules about such vows: the first is that vows should not be made hastily (Prov. 20:25); and the second is that when they are made, they are to be kept (Deut. 23:22-23). This is exactly the Preacher's point. 'Praise awaits you, O God, in Zion;' says the psalmist, 'to you our vows will be fulfilled' (Ps. 65:1, NIV). Worship and covenant-keeping are inextricably bound up in the experience of being a believer.

Vows are to be kept without delay (5:4)

Promises are supposed to be kept. You would never know this from the way most people will say so seriously that they will do one thing, and then, with hardly a blink, do nothing about it. If challenged, they will mutter something about 'forgetting' and 'I meant to do that.' Often, this is followed with as much inactivity as before. You've done it yourself often enough, so you feel too compromised to make much of it — unless you are a manager and you can fire the procrastinator!

If anything, it is the promises made directly to God that fare the worst. But not to keep a vow made to God is the action of a fool, says Solomon (5:4). Why a fool? Because God takes us at face value and will hold us to our solemn commitments. He will not tolerate pious language that is no better than a smoke screen for a deceitful heart and a treacherous hand. It is a fool who trifles with divine righteousness and thinks that God will wink at hypocrisy as if it is no more than a childhood prank!

Vows are to be made carefully (5:5-6)

Hence it is better not to make a vow at all, than to make one and not keep it (5:5). It is too easy to make big promises in the flush of some emotional experience: 'Do not let your mouth cause your flesh to sin!' But it is not good enough to wriggle out of a solemn vow, as if it were no more significant than changing the times of an appointment with the dentist. Why should we incur so lightly the just anger of God (5:6)?

What is crucial here is, once again, the character of God and our personal relationship to him. At first glance, it may seem harsh for God to hold people to their vows. We are so used to broken promises that we tend to shrug them off with a bit of grumbling. We are often surprised when we find someone who is consistently conscientious and trustworthy. A society that takes for granted the easy making and breaking of promises naturally finds God's standards of uprightness rather hard to take. And that is just the point the Preacher wants to get across: God is holy and cannot look upon sin, and those who are truly his believing people *want to do his will* from the depths of their renewed hearts! Believers hate sin and love righteousness. Their

Covenanting with God

William Guthrie (1620-65), in his classic little book on saving faith, *The Christian's Great Interest,* *encourages Christians to engage in personal covenanting with God. 'This explicit [i.e. written] covenant is as an instrument taken of what passed between God and the soul, and so has its own advantage for strengthening of faith.' He was careful to say that this was no different from simply believing in Christ and receiving God's covenant in one's heart. Neither was it something necessary for salvation. Also, it would be of no use apart from 'a sincere heart-closing with God in Christ joined with it' (p. 169). But he notes that, in Scripture, believers often covenant with God in words full of personal commitment confessing the Lord to be their God and that this solemnly strengthens them in their love for God and their witness before the world.

Guthrie points out that God and his Son, Jesus, are perfectly precise and clear in their covenant to save sinners. 'Shall the Lord be so express, plain and peremptory in every part of the business, and shall our part of it rest in a confused thought, and we be as dumb as beasts before Him' (p. 172).

In other words, it is a useful exercise to sit down and write out, in a few sentences, a statement of your commitment to the God and Father of the Lord Jesus Christ, to declare your love for Jesus and your intentions as to how you will live for him as his disciple from now on. It need not be fancy, just simple, scriptural and sincerely from the heart.

*William Guthrie, *The Christian's Great Interest* (London: Banner of Truth, 1969 [1658]).

relationship with God does not consist of a set of external rituals and forms of words, but of heart commitment that results in practical holiness. Believers *love* God and rejoice to do his will. God is good. He is full of grace. He keeps mercy for thousands but will by no means clear the guilty. He calls us to say what we mean and mean what we say. We have promises to keep.

Vows are made before the awesome God (5:7)

Samuel Nesdoly recalls worshipping in the famous Moscow Baptist Church some years ago: 'Especially touching was the message by an eighty-four-year-old saint. He reminded us, that for the Christian, fear of God involved the fear born of love: fear lest we should grieve our loving Heavenly Father.'[2] This is exactly the right side of the Preacher's statement of the alternatives: 'For in the multitude of dreams and many words there is also vanity. But fear God' (5:7).

God is awesome. Before him, all the empty words and false assurance of empty religion will melt away. Ananias and Sapphira discovered that to be the case when they promised God one thing and then did another. Their deaths under the direct judgement of God stand as a monument in the New Testament age (as was the transformation of Lot's wife into a pillar of salt in the Old Testament period) to the impossibility of lying to God and thereby attempting to squeeze into God's kingdom with an unchanged heart and one's sins

intact (Acts 5:1-11; Gen. 19:26; cf. Luke 17:32). Formalistic religion is meaningless before the Lord.

God is, however, awesome in his love. And he draws forth a loving response from all who, having received the Lord Jesus Christ as their Saviour, know him as their Father-God who loved them and chose them 'before the foundation of the world, that we should be holy and without blame before him' (Eph. 1:4). And his love will not let us go. Living worship is simply the life of God in our hearts pouring forth: here in adoration and praise, there in confession of sin and tears of repentance; now in prayer for a deep concern, again in songs of thanksgiving for new life in Christ! Therefore stand in awe of God!

DISCUSS IT

QUESTIONS FOR DISCUSSION

1. What are the two basic rules for voluntary vows (5:4; see also Prov. 20:25; Deut. 23:22-23)?

2. Why is it better not to vow at all, than to make a vow and not keep it (5:5-6)?

3. How are we to relate to God (5:7; see also Luke 17:32; Acts 5:1-11; John 3:16; Eph. 1:14)?

4. How is he to be worshipped (John 4:24)?

CHAPTER ELEVEN

THE LOVE OF MONEY

BIBLE READING

Ecclesiastes 5:8-17

From the problems of empty, purposeless lives and hollow, formalistic religion, the Preacher very naturally turns to the love of money and good things. If we need a reason for living (purpose) and if we have a need for spiritual assurance in the living of life (religion) — and these can easily be the subject of delusion and meaninglessness under the sun — then our desire to sustain and enjoy our daily life (money, wealth) is also bound to hold great potential for under-the-sun meaninglessness. The Preacher is not opposed to wealth (as he makes clear in 5:18-20), but he warns against materialism in all its forms. It is as empty and meaningless as every other tenet of secular (under-the-sun) humanist faith.

He wants us to see how false is the notion that wealth in itself is meaningful — a real answer to life's problems. Looking at it another way, there is an assumption abroad in the world that satisfaction may be found in wealth and that aspiring after greater riches is a good, normal, healthy activity. Certainly, no one would ever deny that an increase in personal income will relieve financial pressure (assuming it does not become an excuse for increasing expenditure and thereby sustaining or even increasing that financial pressure). Neither will anyone deny that material prosperity is a legitimate goal of work. Scripture sees such success as a blessing from God, although it also defines wealth as a stewardship under God, given so that it may be used to further God's work in the world. The general attitude to moneymaking in our society has little room for the biblical stewardship-blessing model of personal prosperity.

The thought of getting something for nothing is far more exciting. It is not a simple desire to escape subsistence that makes gambling — including governmentsponsored lotteries — so popular in the most affluent countries in the world. It is not a burning passion to be enabled to support missionaries at home and abroad that causes, for example, American hearts to beat faster when the $10 million Publisher's Sweepstakes advertisement offer arrives in the mail! (The voice-over ditty on their TV advertisement goes, 'Miracles can happen; they can happen to you/Ten million dollars out of the blue.') Instant wealth seems to promise instant happiness. It is a heady and intoxicating illusion, but its fruit partakes of the same substance as its root. 'Easy come' becomes 'easy go'!

The idea of working for yourself, succeeding, and living what is so deceptively called 'the good life', is equally exciting. It also has a genuine element of legitimate, even laudable, achievement to it, because God does call us to work and he does bless work with

success. But human sin can turn gold to dross and make blessings into curses. Material prosperity, which starts out to be a blessing, can become a tyranny that casts a dark shadow over human lives. What is *good* can so easily become a *god*. And when that happens, *material* becomes an *-ism*.

Distress (5:8-9)

The Preacher begins his development of this theme with a characteristically dark observation on the perennial truth that 'the rich get richer and the poor get poorer'. He notes that where the poor are oppressed, the bureaucracy and the judiciary turn a blind eye. Then they and the king succeed in enriching themselves at the expense of the poor (5:8-9). It is all here: 'justice and rights denied' (v. 8) and ascending tiers of officialdom all making poor excuses to the pleading victim and then passing on a share of the proceeds to shifty-eyed superiors. The punch line is 'do not marvel at the matter' (v. 8). What else can you expect in a world where people live in disregard of the things of God? What else can secularism produce? It has no absolutes outside of itself. At best, it has the shifting-sand relativism of the fifty-one per cent vote and 'public opinion' to render judgement on the currently acceptable moral standards.

An old English music-hall song summed up the poverty of Victorian Britain — then the richest and biggest economy in the world — with that cheerful resentment so characteristic of the British working class:

> It's the same the whole world over;
> > It's the poor wot gets the blame.
> It's the rich wot gets the plunder;
> > Ain't it all a bloomin' shame?

Behind this ditty is a down-to-earth, if cynical and self-serving, philosophy of life. Yes, it's a shame the way things are, but don't look for anything to change. The poor carry the country on their virtuous, hard-working, exploited shoulders, but virtue doesn't pay the rent, so who wants to be poor? The rich are bloodsucking parasites on society, who get the 'plunder' that really belongs to the rest of us, a share of which we are entitled to, and which would obviously make our lives more enjoyable — or, to be pompous about it, more 'meaningful'!

This begs plenty of questions, but there are some grains of truth in it. Being poor is not a virtue, and the oppression of the poor is indeed a shameful, evil thing. The Bible says much about poverty and the poor. Nowhere does it romanticize poverty into a sort of means of grace, as if poverty in itself commended sinners to God and eased their way into heaven by conferring some kind of merit upon them. What the Bible does speak about is that the poor and oppressed will find God to be their helper, when they turn to him in faith

and seek his help in their troubles. And God will certainly judge all human sin and punish those who exploit and oppress their fellow human beings. Furthermore, God calls his people to minister, practically and self-sacrificially, to those who are in need.

Solomon hates injustice but he is totally realistic about the destructive potential of under-the-sun secularism. He 'pins no hopes on utopian

The most famous question asked of Jesus

It was a man who had 'everything' who asked Jesus, 'Good Teacher, what shall I do to inherit eternal life?' (Luke 18:18). It was good that he asked the question — millions never do — but there are clues in it that suggest he already had the answer he wanted to hear.

1. Can you unpack the question and pick out what this fellow meant? (Three key words: 'Good,' 'do' and 'inherit'.)

2. Jesus' answer (Luke 18:19-23) tells him, 'You still lack one thing' and directs him to give away his money. What 'one thing' is Jesus talking about?

3. Identify Jesus' lessons for his disciples and the rest of us (Luke 18:24-30) and set down what he says about riches, heaven and the power and promises of God.

schemes or on revolution. He knows what is in man'.[1]
There is more than a suggestion here that the kind of
motivation that drives people on to self-aggrandizement
and a consuming passion for money inevitably multiplies misery and escalates excess. Is there a real prospect of materialism giving birth to lasting happiness
in this world? Solomon says, in effect, 'Don't hold your
breath!'

Dissatisfaction (5:10-12)

He now goes on to give us three very clear reasons why
more money will never bring more true happiness —
why it is not true, as that American bumper-sticker
states, that 'He who has the most toys wins.'

1. Never enough (5:10)

'He who loves silver will not be satisfied with silver'
(5:10). It is the getting, not the mere having, that is
exciting. What we have is not enough. The fun, the
kudos, the satisfaction, are in the act of acquiring what
our heart desires. As in the days of the prophet Amos,
we have to drink out of bigger and better cups and go
to sleep on more expensive beds (Amos 6:4-6). That
modern barometer of economic success, the standard
of living, is not a fixed point, but a moving gravy
train, which, for those who are on it, must keep on
rolling.

2. Always a bore (5:11)

Success is an anticlimax. When you finally acquire the things you want, they so often become a bore. You may own a Goya or a Gauguin, but you can only 'see them with [your] eyes' — enjoyable, no doubt, but hardly the quintessence of a meaningful life. Furthermore, 'When goods increase, they increase who eat them' (5:11). There are Hollywood stars who have scores of people in their entourage to help them cope with the demands of superstardom. Success always necessitates the recruitment of a staff to administer the growing establishment and its assets. This tends to take the gilt off the gingerbread. Expenses and overheads increase. Profit margins decline in relation to gross income. Wealth has its own burdens.

3. No real security (5:12)

Neither does wealth provide true security. Sir William Burrell (1861-1958) was a Scottish ship owner who devoted most of his long life to amassing a truly marvellous collection of art objects of all types and from all periods. A visit to the Burrell Collection, housed in a beautiful gallery in Pollok Park, Glasgow, is a most memorable excursion through world cultural history. Sir William gave his collection to his native city, but was never to see it on permanent public view. He lived out his latter years as a recluse in his home, Hutton Castle, in mortal fear of fire and theft consuming his life's work. The burden of his consuming passion was the torment of its manifest vulnerability. 'The abundance of the rich,' says the Preacher, 'will not permit him to sleep!' (5:12).

Jesus taught his disciples to put things — and he meant things that are good in themselves — in a divine perspective. Don't store up 'treasures on earth', he said. After all, they are subject to decay and to theft. Rather, 'store up for yourselves treasure in heaven, where moth and rust do not destroy, and where thieves do not break in and steal. For where your treasure is, there your heart will be also' (Matt. 6:19-21, NIV). Notice that this is not a proscription but a prescription. Earthly treasures had a place, but in perspective to their true value. In an under-the-sun outlook, overestimating material prosperity is unavoidable, because to a secular humanist, there is no heaven in which to store up the spiritual treasures that Jesus had in mind in the Sermon on the Mount. To be an earthbound, under-the-sun humanist means that decay and theft nibble daily at the fragile meaning of your life. It is all you really have until and unless you receive the Saviour who is Christ the Lord.

Disaster (5:13-17)

On 19 October 1987, for ever after called 'Black Monday', the New York stock market lost twenty-three per

cent of its paper value. A week or so later, Arthur Kane walked into an office in Miami, pulled a .357 magnum from his briefcase, killed the manager, maimed a broker, and committed suicide. The crash had all but wiped out a multi-million-dollar portfolio, which he had built up through clever speculation, but largely with borrowed funds. When Wall Street plunged, it imploded both the underpinnings of Kane's opulent life-style and, quite clearly, the very fabric of his being.[2]

Materialism is not merely a theory or a life-style, which, like a brand of coffee or a make of washing machine, is morally neutral and physically harmless. Materialism maims and kills. It has consequences that the Preacher describes as 'severe' evils.

1. Is hoarding harmless? (5:13)

One man may hoard his wealth. This is to the 'hurt' of its owner (5:13). But what is that hurt? The text does not spell it out for us, but it gives us a clue — the notion of hoarding. If you ask your average miser why he hoards his wealth, he will tell you that he is not hoarding but saving. He is just being prudent in conserving his assets. Well, is there a substantive distinction between hoarding and saving? Or is it purely a matter of one man's meat being another man's poison? The biblical answer is defined by the

purpose of wealth itself. Why does God give prosperity
to people? Just so that we might, from our bounty, supply the needs of those who are truly poor (2 Cor. 8:13-
15). Money and goods are God's provision for our sus-
tenance, but for the Christian who has such wealth they
are also a channel of God's love that reaches out toward others. Biblical saving is never an end in itself,
but a means toward a loving, outward-reaching end —
that is, provision for real needs. Parents, for example,
should save up for their children and not children for
their parents (2 Cor. 12:14).[3] Saving has definite God-
honouring goals. The channelling, not the immobil-
ization, of resources is in view. Saving takes its place
in the spectrum of a dynamic scriptural spectrum of
Christ-centred personal financial goals, which must
include obedience in the areas of personal consumption, family support, giving to the Lord's church (tith-
ing), debt (minimization and avoidance), and long-term
provision (saving).[4] Saving is one component among
many — and not one that dominates — in a life that is
constrained and guided by a balance of biblical direction for the whole life. Hoarding, in contrast, is the
heresy of which saving is the orthodoxy. The hoarder
serves his hoard, the biblical saver serves his Lord!

The hoarder locks up resources that belong ultimately to God. He keeps them from God and, therefore,
he keeps them from their true purpose. He is willing to
starve men and women to keep his wealth intact. And,
ironically, he even keeps them from himself! Misers
are miserable!

2. What if you lose it all? (5:14)

What about the loss of wealth through some misfortune? This happens and it is a catastrophe for all involved, including the next generation. We expect progress, however modest; we find any drop in our standard of living a bitter pill at the best of times. Having to tighten our belts because of financial strictures is always a tremendous challenge. But what if the goal of our life is embodied in our wealth? What if all we hold dear is tied to our material prosperity? In that case, to lose it is to lose the central motive of life! You have nothing! Your children have nothing! You are lost and your life has come apart at the seams! The Preacher is pleading for some candid stock-taking. Will you, as the devotional writers of past centuries used to put it, 'lie light' to the things of this world? Are you willing to be poorer than you are, and still praise God for it? Are you willing to die to the messianic pretensions of wealth?

3. Does wealth bring real gain? (5:15-17)

Death is the great *terminus ad quem* (the point at which something ends) of Mammon's illusory comforts. 'As he came from his mother's womb, naked shall he return, to go as he came; and he shall take nothing from his labour which he may carry away in his hand' (5:15; cf. vv. 16-17). He takes *something* — his heart, spirit, soul, conscience and character; his relationship with God, whether for weal or woe — but he can take nothing in his *hand*. Shrouds don't have pockets! To live for wealth is simply futile. Where is the gain? He 'eats in darkness' and there is 'much sorrow, sickness and anger!' (5:17). The Preacher's assessment of the blandishments of materialism is, as Charles Bridges remarks, 'a frowning cloud'.[5]

In the parable of the sower, Jesus says that the seed sown among thorns 'is he who hears the word ... and the *deceitfulness* of riches chokes the word, and he becomes unfruitful' (Matt. 13:22). Why does our Lord say this? Surely it is because wealth promises more than it can deliver. Children, when approaching Christmas or a birthday, will vehemently insist that such-and-such toy is exactly what they need. They will assure us that it will really satisfy them. And we all know how ephemeral that satisfaction is. Two days after the opening of the presents, they are back to their old tried and tested playthings. We adults are perhaps more sophisticated in our tastes. We are practised technicians in the quest for personal satisfaction. We are often able to articulate our most naked ambitions in the language of need and even altruism. This is where the 'deceitfulness' attaches itself to the 'riches'. The deceit is in the human heart, of course, and it consists in the notion that a particular level of wealth, or a specific acquisition, will confer a lasting satisfaction of heart and soul. But, as we all know, there is never a complete stamp collection, a perfect house, the best vacation ever, or a large enough multinational corporation. Today's goal becomes tomorrow's baseline. Unhallowed ambition never stops hustling. The carrot is always ahead of the donkey. Satisfaction is an *ignis fatuus* — a 'will o' the wisp'. And the fellow who is chasing it through increased wealth is, as W. G. T. Shedd once said, 'trying to jump off his own shadow … the further he leaps, the further his shadow falls'.[6] If we believe that throwing money at the problem of life will actually give it meaning, forget it! Remember what Jesus said about the deceitfulness of wealth and rather do 'the work of God' — that is, that which endures to eternal life. 'What shall we do, that we may work the works of God?' asked the disciples! 'Jesus answered and said to them, "This is the work of God, that you believe in him whom he sent"' (John 6:28-29).

QUESTIONS FOR DISCUSSION

1. What happens to so much of the fruit of honest toil (5:8-9)? Why is wealth deceitful (Matt. 13:22)?

2. Can materialism give lasting happiness (5:10-12)? Discuss the three answers in these verses and compare them with Matthew 6:19-21.

3. Is materialism a 'victimless' pursuit (5:13-14)? Compare hoarding with the Bible's view of using wealth (2 Cor. 8:13ff; 12:14).

4. What basic truths put wealth in balanced perspective (5:15-17)?

DISCUSS IT

CHAPTER TWELVE

ALTERNATIVES

BIBLE READING

Ecclesiastes 5:18 - 6:12

INTRODUCTION

Solomon frequently, even pervasively, employs a 'reverse psychology' in his presentations of life's challenges. You can see this at work in 5:8-17 when he talks about the emptiness of the love of money. It is as if he is a complete cynic, as if life never rises above the level of living under a cloud of meaningless toil that is going nowhere. He does not, of course, believe this is how life is bound to be.

The Preacher's reverse psychology now takes us from that 'frowning cloud' to the 'bright vision', which is in fact his personal testimony.[1] His emphasis is vibrant with life. The Revised Standard Version accurately renders the Hebrew text: 'Behold, what I have seen to be good and to be fitting is...' (5:18). He commands our attention. 'Hear this,' he says; 'this is what you need to grasp!'

The basic principle: Life is to be enjoyed (5:18-20)

The key word in the Preacher's argument is the name of God. God has given us 'the days of [our] life' (5:18). He has given wealth and the ability to enjoy it (5:19). He gives happiness in our work (5:19). God sustains his people with 'the joy of [their] heart[s]' (5:20). To receive the gift for what it is presupposes believing and trusting in the Giver. The godless enjoyment of the good gifts of God's world is an empty parody of the blessings experienced by the Lord's people as they glory in the goodness of their heavenly Father. 'All things are yours,' says Paul to the Christians in Corinth, 'whether … things present or things to come — all are yours. And you are Christ's, and Christ is God's' (1 Cor. 3:21-22; cf. 1 Tim. 4:3-5). The Christian exults, 'This is my Father's world. He has sent Jesus to be my Saviour. He has given me eternal life and I shall never perish. And he provides for me every day with his goodness. Praise God, from whom all blessings flow! Praise him, all creatures here below. Praise him above you heavenly host! Praise Father, Son, and Holy Ghost!'

One of the great misconceptions that many, including some very sincerely committed Christians, entertain about the Christian life is the notion that it is supposed to be rather sombre and sorrowful. Some years ago, during the question time after one of the presentations at a pastor's study conference, the speaker somehow took us from the necessity of reverence in worship to a blanket condemnation of smiling during a service! For him, the only proper attitude for the worship of God was an unrelieved seriousness, if not indeed strickenness, of both spirit and visage! Regrettably, this pastor has not been alone in this opinion. Like dripstone forming in a limestone cave, this straitened joylessness has — unintentionally, no doubt — built up a cold calcified overlay on the lives of many Christians such that they feel inhibited about enjoying the good gifts of God and giving vent to it in his praise.

Scripture teaches the exact opposite. The Lord turns mourning into dancing for those he saves from their sins. He calls us to rejoice in his gifts. We are promised that there is real satisfaction for us in our labour, however toilsome it may be. He rolls back the effects of man's fall into sin — the curse of Genesis 3:17 — and redeems the whole life of his people. He sent his only-begotten Son to die an atoning, substitutionary death for the sins of every sinner that he will save for himself. Rejoicing is the *only* appropriate response and ought to pervade every aspect of the Christian's devotion to the Lord. Sometimes there will be tears, but they will be out of joy as well as grief.

Challenge 1: Count the cost (6:1-6)

Think about what you lose when you go the world's way. God actually showers his gifts upon people of all sorts and conditions. There is a common goodness of God to the human race whom he created to be his image-bearers in the world. Many people have their heart's desire (6:2). The rich young ruler and the eponymous antiheroes of the parables of the rich fool, and the rich man and Lazarus are clear examples of this in the New Testament (Luke 18:18-30; 12:13-34; 16:19-31). For many, there is something missing. They never quite get to enjoying it as they would like. The Preacher attributes this to the hand of God (6:2). Sometimes their wealth falls to a stranger (6:2). Another has many children, but is so reviled by them that he is not even accorded a decent burial (6:3).

Surely, says the Preacher, this is meaningless. Here you are, living out your life under the sun — no God, no future beyond the grave, no certainties in this life, except its uncertainties and its shortness, and plenty of pain and frustration in the meantime. A stillborn child is better off! It comes and goes and is forgotten; and in under-the-sun terms it has more peace than the fellow who slaves away for years — even supposing he lived 2,000 years — yet fails to enjoy his prosperity (6:4-6)!

The argument is relentless and irrefutable. We all know that if this life is all there is, then it is undeniable that the billionaire and the stillborn baby 'all go to one

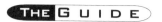

place' (6:6). Death ends whatever meaning there might have been. Is this the basis on which you want to live out your days? Is this all that you

The joy of holiness

Jerry Bridges points out that 'God intends the Christian life to be a life of joy — not drudgery. The idea that holiness is associated with a dour disposition is a caricature of the worst sort. In fact, the opposite is true. Only those who walk in holiness experience true joy.'*

1. Joy flows from particular experiences and exercises in our lives. Identify these from the following passages:

John 15:10-11
Psalm 16:11 (cf. Ps. 51:12)
Hebrews 12:1-2 (cf. Matt. 25:21,23)

2. True joy gives form and direction to the new life of the Christian.

Nehemiah 8:10
Romans 14:17

Only a heart renewed by God's grace enjoys personal holiness.
Christians ought to be the happiest people in the world. Are you one of them?

* Jerry Bridges, *The Pursuit of Holiness* (Colorado Springs: Navpress, 1978), p. 154ff.

can make of the world around you? Is this your response to the manifest evidence of God's existence, goodness, and claims upon your life?

Challenge 2: Are you satisfied? (6:7-12)

The writer has been reflecting on three significant problems relative to the meaning of life — a general feeling of purposelessness in life (4:1-16), the hollowness of formalistic religion (5:1-7), and the futility and frustration of a materialistic love of money and things (5:8 - 6:6). Obviously, this is neither a systematic nor a comprehensive treatment of the problems confronting human society. It is sufficient, however, to get people thinking, and that is the Preacher's purpose. If we will but face a few facts in the light of God's gracious plan and purpose to redeem human lives from self-destruction and eternal loss, then will not every thought become captive to the Saviour as the realization of truth is applied progressively to every aspect of our lives?

In this postlude, therefore, Solomon wafts some of the leading thoughts of his three-chapter passage on problems across the (hopefully) agitated waters of our minds. It is as if he is saying: 'Think on these things! Don't let them escape. Don't shrink from the issues. Wrestle with them and, as Jacob wrestled with God at Peniel (Gen. 32:22ff.), refuse to let them go without a blessing and a happy resolution.'

Review the implications of under-the-sun life. The purpose of our endless work still seems elusive. On the face of it, our physical appetite dictates what we do, and yet we never get to the point where it is satisfied. We have to keep on keeping on ... apparently for ever (6:7)! In the end, does the wisdom of the Ph.D. really make him any better off than the uneducated peasant (6:8)? No, says the Preacher, 'Better is the sight of the eyes [that is, the enjoyment of the real gifts God has given to us] than the wandering of desire [the chasing of unhallowed and unsatisfiable desires]' (6:9).

The truth is that the human thirst for autonomy over against God is a phantasm (6:10-12). There is 'one who is mightier than [we],' with whom we 'cannot contend' (6:10). Who can dispute with God? 'Woe to him who strives with his Maker,' thundered the prophet. 'Shall the clay say to him who forms it, "What are you making?"' (Isa. 45:9). Our limitations are so obvious that any pretensions to godlike autonomy are almost laughable. The more we talk, the less meaningful are our words. 'Who knows what is good...?' (6:12). Under-the-sun man has no absolutes to guide him. Take away G-O-D and 'good' becomes a big round O — there is no standard except the most recently triumphant philosophical and ethical fad. And how long will that last? As to the future, 'Who can tell a man what will happen?' (6:12). There are no certainties either. No promises. No milestones along the way to the non-existent goals of this under-the-sun world. Only fears about pollution, the ozone layer, global warming, nuclear war, third world debt, and the economy. What can you really live for if that is the way of things? What value is your wealth in such a context? The Preacher 'is slamming every door except the door of faith'.[2] In the fulness of New Testament revelation, Paul would tell the apostolic church that 'the Scripture declares that the whole world is a prisoner of sin, so that what was promised, being given through faith in Jesus Christ, might be given to those who believe' (Gal. 3:22, NIV). There is just no other way.

QUESTIONS FOR DISCUSSION

1. *Identify two alternatives to materialism in 5:18 - 6:6 and discuss what this implies for the way we are to live our lives.*

2. *What does Solomon think about this (6:7-11)?*

3. *Discuss what you found in the 'Think about…' box on the joy of the Christian life.*

CHAPTER THIRTEEN

HARD
EXPERIENCES

BIBLE READING

Ecclesiastes 7:1-6

INTRODUCTION

Hitherto, the Preacher's focus has been very much on the dark side of the world's problems — specifically, lack of purpose (4:1-23), formalistic religion (5:1-7), and materialism (5:8 - 6:12). Now he addresses himself to the answers we so desperately need. He begins with a series of proverbs, in which he successively speaks of the value of hard experiences (7:1-6), potential hindrances to spiritual growth (7:7-10), and the need of a God-centred wisdom to cope with life (7:11-14).

Experience is a great teacher, it is said. Alas, even the greatest of teachers have run up against some less-than-great learners! These are not necessarily in the minority either. There is little evidence that mankind is breaking out of his long-standing habit of repeating the mistakes of the past. It sometimes seems as if every generation has, so to speak, to 'reinvent the wheel' in terms of public morals and personal ethics. The appreciation of the lessons of history — history is, after all, the only real mediator between past mistakes and present decision-making — does not come very naturally to the young and the restless. When we are young we are looking to gain experience for ourselves and we tend to be impatient with the advice of our elders. We too easily imagine that we will do things properly. We boldly comfort ourselves with the thought that, should we stumble and fall, this would only be par for the course. Don't we all have to make our own mistakes anyway?

Wise and experienced elders may become a little agitated at such attitudes. But youthful inexperience aside, there is a core of truth in this position, for it remains a fact of life that we learn many, if not most, of our best lessons through our personal and often painful experiences of setback and failure. It must also be admitted, however, that this is often a case of learning the hard way! And it surely goes without saying that ignoring the lessons that may be gleaned from the experiences of others is hardly a wise way to proceed in life.

This theme — learning from experience, and in particular, responding to the hard things in life — is taken up in Ecclesiastes 7:1-6. Nowhere in human experience is there a wider gap between theory and practice than in the way we respond to personal difficulties. It is so easy to trot out some quaint piece of bravado like 'When the going gets tough, the tough get going' — especially when somebody else has been hit by a serious problem — only to crumble into a crushed paralysis of spirit when we ourselves are waylaid by a personal setback. We all want everything to go smoothly and easily.

Such an aspiration is thoroughly biblical and is a very appropriate focus of our prayers for ourselves and others. 'Make it your ambition,' said the apostle Paul, 'to lead a quiet life, to mind your own business ... so that your daily life may win the respect of outsiders' (1 Thess. 4:11-12, NIV). Nevertheless, there are certain givens about life in the real world — and one of them is that sooner or later we will run into something that is neither of our choosing nor to our liking. If we are to respond positively to these difficulties, if and when they arise, we will need to be prepared for them. At the very least, we will need to be persuaded that there is some possibility of redeeming such experiences so that defeats may be turned into victories.

Funerals are better than birthdays! (7:1-4)

The first of Solomon's two examples is, not surprisingly perhaps, that most inevitable of inconveniences in life ... death. He begins with a most amazing statement: 'A good name is better than precious ointment, and the day of death than the day of one's birth' (7:1). Our immediate response is to ask what, if anything, these two sayings have to do with one another. They seem to be entirely unrelated ideas, at least to Westerners. To the Hebrew, however, there was a rich parallel in the conjunction of these seemingly disparate thoughts. To have a good name is better than a fine perfume (that is what the 'ointment' in the text is) because the former represents something of the inward essential nature of a person — reputation and integrity. Perfume, on the other hand, is just on the surface — an often delightful but essentially outward and cosmetic effect. To reverse the image, I am reminded of a Scotsman's comment on a hopelessly over-made-up woman: 'If it takes that much manure,' he cracked, 'it cannae be verry great soil underneath!' A good name tells us something real about the person; whereas perfume only masks reality with a superficial and transient aroma. In a similar way, the Preacher is suggesting that the 'day of death' is better than 'the day of one's birth'. Why? Because the day of death — not just the future day when we each pass into eternity, but the repeated days of bereavement we go through when loved ones and dear friends die — focuses our minds on the crucial, ultimate questions of the meaning of life and the prospect of eternity. It is not that remembering birthdays and having birthday parties are bad things — not at all! It is just that, in the face and prospect of death, our minds are, if we let them, concentrated on the most basic realities of our lives. Paradoxically perhaps, it is death that reaches into our deepest being and moulds the very pattern of future life, while birth represents a backward-looking sentiment, devoid of power to channel what we will do with the years that are left to us.

This calls for explanation for the obvious reason that it is not self-evident that funerals are better than

THINK ABOUT IT

THINK ABOUT IT

Death and religion, Hollywood style

The 1971 movie *The Omega Man* is set in post-biological warfare holocaust Los Angeles. Among the few survivors are mutated dying humans organized in religious brotherhood, dressed like monks and led by 'Brother Matthias' (Anthony Zerbe), and a gun-toting scientist 'Robert Neville' (Charlton Heston), eventually joined by a multiethnic mix of children and young adults. The twist is that the 'baddies' are the religionists, who are essentially a death cult, while the 'goodies' are the life-loving secularists led by the scientist, who dies, arms outstretched and bleeding into the water of a fountain, while the young folks head off with a vial of his blood — the cure for the lethal mutations that killed everybody else — to build the new humanity in the Sierra. Redemption through science triumphs over death by religion. The blood of messianic scientific naturalism cleanses from all religious irrationalism! The 'Omega' man is the sci-fi 'fountain opened for uncleanness' who saves humanity, while Jesus the God-man, the true Fountain and the actual 'Alpha and Omega' (Rev. 1:8; 22:13) is absent and irrelevant. The Bible is turned on its head. Death is from God. Life is in us, just waiting to be discovered.

How is death treated in more modern movies? What lessons are being taught? Is the 'spirituality' of the twenty-first century an advance on the secularism of the twentieth? How has New Age mysticism affected how people think about death? The Bible distinguishes three types of death: physical (Rom. 5:12; 6:23), spiritual (Eph. 2:1) and eternal (Matt. 8:12; 10:28; 25:41).* What does this tell us about our greatest need?

*Eryl Davies, *Heaven is a Far Better Place* (Darlington: Evangelical Press, 1999), pp. 28-33.

birthdays! Death is the very thing from which we naturally shrink. The Preacher offers two explanations.

1. How death helps us to think about life (7:2).

This is the principal value of funerals, and you will
notice that it is also the antithesis of a merely morbid
introspection. It is the opposite of the satanic preoccupation with death so pervasive in the horror and
science-fiction genres of movies and literature. Bereavement calls the thoughtless to think about realities in a
way that parties and fun never will. Death knocks away
the props and planks with which people shore up their
empty lives. Death reminds us of the realities that at
other times we succeed in blotting out of our minds.
And this is because 'every funeral anticipates our own'.[1]
From this perspective, the tragically unwelcome
intruder also carries an overture of grace from the outstretched hand of God. It is his grace that takes the devastating evil that death is in itself and lays it on our
hearts in such a way as to make us think … perhaps
bring us to pray out of a sense of our need … and even
bring us to fellowship with Jesus Christ, who died to
kill death for all who would simply believe in him as
their Saviour.

To be ready to die is to be ready for life and living.
This is why Paul could say, 'For to me, to live is Christ
and to die is gain' (Phil. 1:21). What is his argument? It
is just this: because he is ready to die, in Christ, and
that would be eternal gain, so his whole life can be
wonderfully lived out in discipleship to his risen

Saviour. This is the central glorious paradox of the Christian life. Make me a captive, Lord, and then I shall be free! The first shall be last and the last shall be first. He that is least in the kingdom of heaven shall be the greatest, and he that is greatest, the servant of all. In the midst of death we see life. His — Jesus' — strength is made perfect in our weakness. 'Dying,' said the apostle Paul, 'we live.' The Preacher is in perfect harmony with the universal teaching of Scripture, when he says, 'Better to go to the house of mourning than to go to the house of feasting, for that is the end of all men; and the living will take it to heart' (7:2).

2. How sorrow can deepen our innermost being (7:3-4).

Again we see the paradox — true happiness and joy are deepened and developed through the sorrows we may undergo. The point is not that we should be as sad as we possibly can be, as if, like endless doses of castor oil, this will do us a lot of good. There is no virtue in adopting a martyr complex. Sorrows are enemies, not friends. They are the rivulets that flow into the ocean of death. And like death, they must be conquered and turned around to some positive purpose, or they will consume us altogether. There is no need to beg trouble or to create difficulties for ourselves. Those that come along in the normal course of events are sufficient to test our faith. For the child of God, they can be a means of drawing us closer to the Lord. 'Weeping may endure for a night, but joy comes in the morning' (Ps. 30:5). Joy is the redemptive side of sorrow.

Rita Nightingale learned this as she sat in the secluded shade underneath the hospital building in Lard Yao prison in Bangkok (the building was on stilts). Rita had been imprisoned after drugs were found in luggage she was carrying for a boyfriend. In the despair and discomfort of that Thai jail, she was led to faith in Christ. She had bitterly complained about the injustice of men and God in bringing her to such a sorry pass. But through the witness of women missionaries who visited her and especially that of Robert Laidlaw's famous tract, *The Reason Why*, given to her by an elderly lady from her home town in England, she came to experience the freedom of the gospel of Christ. She realized that she had left God out of her life and that he, in his great love, had pursued her through the miseries of her imprisonment precisely so that she could be saved from her sins and brought to new life. 'Eventually,' she records, 'I emerged from under the hospital hut and went inside it. I sat down in the waiting area and gazed out across the compound, blinking in the suddenly bright sunlight. It's not just us who are in prison, I suddenly thought. The whole world's in prison, and I've just been shown the way out. I've been in prison all my life.'[2] After reading a borrowed Bible

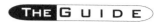
that evening, she could say with simple sincerity of heart, 'I closed the Bible feeling happy. I might not know much about God, but now I knew who he was.'[3]

Rebuke is better than song (7:5-6)

A second major species of personal experience that can be felt most keenly is that of admonition or rebuke. 'The wounds of the soul', writes James W. Alexander, 'are not always such as bleed outwardly, nor is the most poignant anguish caused by visible agents.' When someone rebukes us in any way, he says, 'there is always an emotion of unhappiness'.[4] Even when we know we are in the wrong and are sure that the person is rebuking us in genuine love, we feel the pain. We may be kicking ourselves, but we often feel like lashing out at others as well! It hurts at the best of times!

How are we to deal with such hurt? What does God wish to show us? Surely that we should change our ways. But also that we might value this correction as a privilege and a good gift. 'It is better to hear the rebuke of the wise, than for a man to hear the song of fools' (7:5), says the Preacher. It is better, of course, because wisdom is like gold and ought to be heeded for our own and everybody else's good. But it is better for at least two other reasons.

1. Tough love is good for you

It takes love, as well as wisdom, for a wise man to rebuke someone who is on the skids of error and who may even be careering toward self-destruction. Many a pastor has been praised for his excellent sermons, but none was more encouraged by a parishioner's comment than the preacher who was told by one of his congregation that the thing that had impressed him most forcibly from week to week was the fact that he — the pastor — loved his people so much as to tell them the truth! Such love ought to be returned with loving gratitude. Many years ago, a young man, a student for the gospel ministry, had to deliver a sermon before his presbytery.[5] After he had delivered it, the pastors and elders had opportunity to make comments on it and vote to sustain or not sustain. Generally the comments were positive, but one pastor, while commending the seminarian, remarked that for all that was good and scriptural in the sermon, it had in fact missed the central point of the Bible text. He explained this key concept in a few words and commended it as a point for future consideration. Many years later, the two men — the student was now a pastor of many years experience — ran into one another at a meeting and began reminiscing about years past. 'Do you remember that time when you criticized my sermon before the presbytery?' the second man said. 'I was so angry at the time, it just burned me up to be told I'd missed the point. Well, some years later I decided to preach on that text. So I dusted off my student sermon and read it

over. And as I reviewed it, all that you had said that day came back to me, and as it did, I realized that you had been absolutely correct and my anger had been totally unjustified! Thank you for making such a searching comment, and let me encourage you never to shrink back from telling people what they need to hear from God!' Be thankful for a wise counsellor, for 'Open rebuke is better than love carefully concealed. Faithful are the wounds of a friend, but the kisses of an enemy are deceitful' (Prov. 27:5-6).

2. Consider the alternative

Another, and compelling, reason to listen to the rebuke of a wise counsellor, is that the alternative is bad news. Listening to 'the song of fools' can be great fun, but is hardly a sure-footed guide to unravelling the intricacies of life. The very expression 'the song of fools' conjures up images of the happy hour when the drinks flow and the most threadbare of jokes can raise a roistering laugh. This is like 'the crackling of thorns under a pot' (7:6). There is a Hebrew pun in this expression. The *sirim* (thorns) crackle under the *sir* (pot).[6] And the music of the language takes a tilt at the burning of an inferior fuel — thorns rather than the normal charcoal — that is more sound than substance, more show than solidarity. This represents the character of foolishness and flattery. It warns against the false promises of the easy way out. 'Woe to you who laugh now,' Jesus taught his followers, 'for you shall mourn and weep' (Luke 6:25). Some imagine that they can drown their sorrows and escape from the challenges of life in carousing and conviviality. But after the last hurrah, it's back, as the Scots say, to 'auld claes [clothes] and porridge'. The world is still there. And it won't go away. That is why a rebuke from a wise and loving friend is worth the pain it necessarily inflicts. 'Now no chastening seems to be joyful for the present, but painful; nevertheless, afterward it yields the peaceable fruit of righteousness to those who have been trained by it' (Heb. 12:11).

Because the Bible is the inscripturated revelation of God's Word to mankind, it is the ultimate authority in matters of faith and life. It follows that if more people were to heed it with spiritual discernment and intelligent devotion, there would be more learning through good experiences than bad! But God's Word always reckons with realities. Among these is the fact that we sin and we do stupid things. Another reality is that troubles will come into our lives unbidden by anything we have said or done. God fills our lives with experiences through which he means to teach us and lead us to practical wisdom and spiritual maturity. The Holy Spirit was sent to the New Testament church to be our Helper, Comforter and Counsellor who would lead us into 'all truth' (John 16:13). His work is never a mere intellectual transaction, like learning facts from a text-book, but is a practical course in which he brings the

Word of God to bear upon our real experiences. The world is a school of hard knocks — and God uses it to bring us to Christian maturity.

QUESTIONS FOR DISCUSSION

1. *Why is the day of death better than the day of our birth (7:1). Tie this in with what Paul says in Philippians 1:21 and 2 Corinthians 6:9.*

2. *When are hard words to be regarded as good things (7:5-6; Prov. 27:5-6)?*

3. *What is the basic principle governing the Christian's hard experiences (Rom. 8:28; Heb. 12:11)?*

CHAPTER FOURTEEN

CLEARING HURDLES

BIBLE READING

Ecclesiastes 7:7-14

Some of the most technically unforgiving events in track athletics are the various hurdles and steeplechase races. Hitting the hurdles not only slows you down, but can be painful and discouraging. The hurdlers have to train hard to make sure they clear the hurdles cleanly and quickly. Life is a hurdle race — not 110, 400 or 3,000 metres, but life-long. Of course, on the track, they are utterly predictable. In life, you never know when one will turn up. Sometimes, you only know you hit one when you are trying to pick yourself up after taking a real hard knock. The trouble with 'the school of hard knocks' — that is what the hurdles in life are all about — is that the bruising can too easily crowd out the learning and retard personal growth. Trials can burn us out. Many who followed Jesus at first 'walked no more with him' when trouble came (John 6:66). Setbacks can crush a person's spirit. But to be forewarned is to be powerfully forearmed. Just knowing what is happening to us gives us an opportunity to respond — perhaps to take avoiding action, certainly to pray for God's help.

Hindrances to growth (7:7-10)

The Preacher alerts us to four possible hindrances to personal growth. These are 'pressure', impatience, frustration and vain regrets.

1. Pressure (7:7)

The first may be identified with what we today call pressure. The 'oppression' that 'destroys a wise man's reason' and the 'bribe' that 'debases the heart' (7:7) represent the power other people can exercise to manipulate and dominate us and to wreck our integrity and individuality. Oppression, not excluding temptation to sin, tends to dehumanize in the sense that it enslaves and corrupts its victims. Succumbing to pressure undermines the moral foundations of our convictions and value systems and steadily erodes that sense of balance and proportion with which we order our lives. People under pressure can feel driven to desperate and even suicidal actions. The Preacher's warning is to identify and retreat from pressure as it encroaches on your life.

2. Impatience (7:8)

The second pitfall is an impatient attitude. The Preacher emphasizes that 'the end of a thing is better than its

beginning' (7:8). This is true only of God's good things — in contrast, sin begins sweetly and ends in bitterness. Solomon is looking at the life of commitment to the Lord. His point is that we look at the goal, not at the hurdles we are presently trying to negotiate. The trial of our faith, after all, is designed to produce patience (James 1:2-4) and to result in greater, even eternal, triumph (2 Cor. 4:17; 1 Peter 5:9-10). 'Patience is the child of faith.'[1] Impatience is the illegitimate offspring of self-worship. Hence, the Preacher's contrast: patience is better than pride (7:8). Pride is essentially self-worship. Pride may well get us off to a confident start, but only patience will pull us through the rough spots.

3. Frustration (7:9)

The third danger is perhaps an extension of the foregoing point, namely, the tendency to outrage when things do not go according to plan. We live in a day when outrage is regarded as a virtue. The ski masks worn by demonstrators and rioters of our cities have become the badges of modern righteous indignation. *Not* to raise your fist at the slightest provocation is to risk being regarded as a 'wimp'. And in the media age, the presence of TV cameras virtually assures extravagantly aggressive behaviour from demonstrators. Ours is the age of the short fuse. Litigation at the drop of a hat, violence on the strike picket lines, histrionics in the check-out line, death in the streets; all are the symptoms of a society in which frustration has become the justification for instant vengefulness. That such anger is bound to be counterproductive and can only escalate the cycle of frustration and anger to greater and more lethal intensities is palpably obvious. It is, as the Scriptures repeatedly assert, bound up with foolishness in the human heart (7:9; Prov. 14:17,29; 15:18; 16:32). And James's corrective has urgent relevance: 'let every man be swift to hear, slow to speak, slow to wrath' (James 1:19; cf. Eccles. 7:9).

4. Vain regrets (7:10)

A fourth and final hindrance to learning from our experience is vain regret that harks back to 'the good old days' ('Why were the former days better than these?' 7:10). The Preacher is not saying that history is nonsense. He is not suggesting that the study of history is a bad thing. Neither is he decrying the enjoyment of happy memories of days gone by. What he is concerned about is the kind of discontent that longs to turn back the clock to some alleged golden age in the past. Pining for the glory days, as they imagined them, was one of Israel's recurrent failings — always in times of difficulty. During their wanderings in the Sinai desert, they even longed for their slavery in Egypt (Exod. 16:3; Num. 11:5-6; 14:1-4). Christians are not immune to this temptation. People enmeshed in the convoluted

THINK ABOUT IT

How are we to deal with tough breaks?

In that little gem on the Christian life, *The Crook in the Lot*, *Thomas Boston outlines the method by which hard experiences will bear fruit in our hearts. (The 'lot' is your pathway through life. The 'crook' is a bend in that path — a painful diversion and distraction along the way.)

1. Believe that *God's hand is in it* and that he is sovereign. He encourages us to 'consider it as the work of your God in Christ. This is the way to sprinkle it with Gospel grace... The discerning of a Father's hand in the crook will take out much of the bitterness of it and sugar the pill to you. For this cause it will be necessary (1) Solemnly to take God for your God, under your crook, Psalm 142:4-5. (2) In all your encounters with it, resolutely to believe and claim your interest in Him, 1 Samuel 30:6' (p. 64).

2. Believe that *God is good.* Consider who God is, says Boston, — as 'your Father, elder Brother, Head, Husband, etc., who, therefore, surely consults your good' (p. 64). See Romans 8:28.

3. Believe that *he is teaching you something* — perhaps correcting some sin, preventing some inadvisable course of action, deepening your self-awareness, and moulding your character to be more like Christ. Thomas Watson says of the Lord's chastisements in the Christian life, 'The depth of affliction is to save us from the depth of damnation' (*All Things for Good*, Edinburgh, Banner of Truth, 1998 [1663], p. 62).

* Thomas Boston, *The Crook in the Lot*
(Swengel, Pa., Reiner:1963).[2]

responsibilities of middle life look back to the carefree days of youth or college and the happy camaraderie of a new and wider circle of friends. There are people who never recover from the loss of what they believe were indeed the happiest days of their lives. There are other Christians who long for the excitement of their earliest experiences as new converts to Jesus Christ and feel the rest of their lives to have been an anticlimax. There are whole churches that steep themselves wistfully in their history, in times when they were more influential and seemed to be specially blessed with gospel power.

To think this way, says the Preacher, is unwise (7:10). Why? Simply because past days, however successful, are gone beyond recall. To learn from the past is good, as is the desire for the fulness of God's blessing now and in the future. But to pine after the past is to attempt to live life in reverse. Your real life is now and in the future. Your experience, past and present, must drive you forward to seek the Lord's blessing in the application of lessons learned, not backward to sentimental dreams of vanished joy. God has, after all, given his believing children a personal faith in Christ which, as they receive the goal of their faith, fills them with 'joy inexpressible and full of glory' (1 Peter 1:8). It is this irreducible joy in the heart of the Christian that can enable him to gain the victory over the bad times and the temptations to look back, and come to the place of the apostle who could brush aside the severest troubles as 'light' and 'for a moment' and declare them to

be achieving for him 'a far more exceeding and eternal weight of glory' (2 Cor. 4:17).

Wisdom from God (7:11-14)

God-given wisdom is the key to redeeming the multifaceted experiences of life. As we shall see in the next chapter, the Preacher will show us how this wisdom can be acquired and developed. In the present context, he wants to emphasize that wisdom is a good thing — 'good with an inheritance' — which benefits those 'who see the sun' (7:11). How, in a nutshell, does this work out? Well, says the Preacher, it is a shelter — like, for example, money. You all know how having money can shelter you in a most practical way from nasty things like hunger and cold. Wisdom is like that, only more so, for it 'gives life to those who have it' (7:12). The point is that wisdom is a species of wealth that transcends the under-the-sun world and reaches to heaven. Or, rather, true wisdom reaches *from* heaven, from the Lord, and equips the believer with the resources to live a full and God-honouring life. To underscore this, the Preacher reminds us that our lives are indeed lived under the hand of God (7:13-14). We are back to Ecclesiastes 3 and the biblical doctrine of the providence of God. The base-line presupposition of a faith that centres in the sovereign God is that our life — and the whole world — is in his hand. He knows the end from the beginning; he is absolutely sovereign; and he even marks the fall of a sparrow (Isa. 46:10; Dan. 4:34-35; Matt. 10:29). Our life also follows the arrow of time — from birth to the future. But it is not always a perfectly straight line. It is crooked at points. Sometimes these are little blips and at other times wide detours.

The vital point is that the purpose of God is being worked out in both the straight and the crooked. So the Preacher asks, 'Who can make straight what he has made crooked?' (7:13). God is dealing with us along the whole of our life's path. It follows that when times are good we should 'be joyful' and when problems arise we should 'consider' (7:14). God is doing all things well. His timing is perfect. His goal is the highest possible good for all who love him. If there are bends in our road, they are the 'crooked places' that 'shall be made straight … for the mouth of the LORD has spoken' (Isa. 40:4-5).

QUESTIONS FOR DISCUSSION

1. What four pitfalls are we warned about in 7:7-10?

2. Why do we need wisdom, and where will we find it (7:11-14; see also Isa. 46:10; Dan. 4:34-35; Matt. 10:29)?

3. Discuss the 'Think about…' question: How are we to deal with tough breaks?

CHAPTER FIFTEEN

FACING
REALITY

LOOK IT UP

BIBLE READING

Ecclesiastes 7:15-18

INTRODUCTION

People may run away from problems, but problems never run away from people. The student had a problem. His theology paper was due by noon on Friday, and he hadn't the slightest hope of finishing it in time. So he decided, with lamentable dishonesty, to submit what he had written with some blank pages at the end to simulate the thickness of a completed paper. He would put it on the professor's desk and hope that he would leave the papers there over the weekend without looking at them, beyond noting who had handed them in on time. This had happened on other occasions, so he felt it to be a reasonable risk. First thing on Monday, he would come in early with the missing section and replace the blank pages. By noon that Friday, phase one of the deception was put into operation. The incomplete paper was on the professor's desk. He just hoped the plan would work. Less than an hour later, however, an angry professor tracked him down in the library, demanding not only an explanation for the blank pages, but also slapping a 5 p.m. final deadline for the rest of the paper! His deception in ruins and a serious question mark raised about his personal integrity as a Christian, the student got to work to redeem the extra time he had been given. After a while he just couldn't do any more. He had to take a break. So he slipped out of the building and ducked around the corner to a little coffee shop. As he sat there nursing his coffee, his weariness, and maybe his shame, he looked up ... and who should be coming into the coffee shop, but the professor himself! Even before his mentor spotted him, he was on his feet and running out of the door! But as he passed the astonished teacher, he plaintively (and with an irreverent disregard for its true meaning) muttered the words of the psalmist, 'Whither shall I flee from thy presence!'[1] There was no escape. It was back to hitting the books. He completed the paper and the course. He never entered the ministry.

Evasion will not succeed — the chickens soon come home to roost! Escapism doesn't make the world go away — it is still there after the hangover or the drug trip. Emigration doesn't work — the grass isn't greener on the other side of the hill. Living as a recluse (eremitism) also fails — because bad consciences and favourite temptations will follow the hermit into his retreat. Whatever stratagem is adopted, problems are neither escaped nor resolved by shutting our eyes and hoping they go away.

It is only in facing the facts — on God's terms — that answers can and will be discovered. This is the Preacher's consistent message. And the various threads

of his argument point in the direction of our need of wisdom. Without wisdom we are bound to be thrown back on resources that, in the view of God's Word, are no better than the song or the laughter of fools (7:5-6).

What is wisdom?

A most thought-provoking definition of wisdom was given by Thomas Manton in a sermon he preached on Jesus' words in Matthew 11:19: 'wisdom is proved right by her actions'. Manton says:

> By wisdom is meant the *doctrine of the gospel,* called elsewhere the *counsel of God,* as appears from the parallel passage in Luke 7:29-30: 'And all the people that heard him justified God, being baptized with the baptism of John. But the Pharisees and lawyers rejected the counsel of God against themselves.' The gospel way of salvation is there called the counsel of God, because it is the counsel he gives to men for their good; as here wisdom, because *it is the result of God's eternal wisdom and decrees.* And elsewhere the doctrine of Christ crucified is called 'the wisdom of God'; and again, 1 Corinthians 2:7: 'the wisdom of God in a mystery'.[2]

WHAT THE TEXT TEACHES

The contours of biblical wisdom are all here: it is revealed in the counsel of God (specifically the death of Jesus Christ, but including the inscripturated Word of God); and it results in the transformation of the lives of men and women as the Holy Spirit brings them to faith in Christ. Biblical wisdom stands in stark contrast with the 'wisdom of this world' — also called in Scripture 'wisdom of words', 'the wisdom of the wise', 'man's wisdom', and 'fleshly wisdom' (1 Cor. 3:19; 1:17,19; 2:4; 2 Cor. 1:12). This is the wisdom of autonomous secular-humanist man who has declared his independence from God. In principle, it rejects the whole idea of a revealed wisdom from God. Not surprisingly, the Scriptures declare it to be 'foolishness with God' (1 Cor. 3:19). It is God who is true wisdom and in relation to whom, through personal faith in Christ, wisdom is embraced and exercised.

When the Preacher speaks of the need of wisdom, it is *God's* wisdom he has in mind. True wisdom is never divorced from the words and work of God. The Preacher is a 'theocentric antiabstractionist'. For him, wisdom is not something abstracted from God, and derived from age, intelligence, or experience *in themselves*. The real wisdom arises from the interaction of the directive, revealed truth of God and the responsive human mind and heart, all under the illuminating influence of the Holy Spirit.

In this perspective, there is no abstract, secularized wisdom that straddles, colossus-like, the supposed common ground between competing faiths. The secular

The joy of fearing God

Jerry Bridges tells how a Christian leader reacted with disbelief to his use of this expression (later to become a book title). 'Christianity means a relationship with God,' he objected, 'but how can you have a relationship with someone you fear?' Bridges goes on to recall that at one time Christians were known as 'God-fearing' and it was counted as a 'badge of honour'.*

Why should it be a *joy* to fear God? Remember that those who do not know God do not have this fear that brings joy (see Ps. 36:1). And until and unless they come to know Christ as their Saviour, the only fear of God they will know is the servile fear of those under God's righteous judgement (Matt. 25:24-25). Look up the verses and note down the reasons.

1. It is where … begins (Prov.1:7; 9:10, cf. John 17:3)

2. It is blessed with God's… (Ps. 31:19)

3. It is evidence of… (Col. 3:22; 2 Cor. 7:1)

4. It is the example of… (Isa. 11:1-3)

5. It keeps us from… (Exod. 20:20; cf. Heb. 12:6)

6. It humbles us to … us in due time (1 Peter 5:6)

* J. Bridges, *The Joy of Fearing God* (Colorado Springs: Waterbrook Press, 1997), p. 1.

notion of wisdom enshrines the self-serving myth that man by searching can find himself to be god,[3] generating his own meaning from the inductive processes of his own mind and experience. If we are truly to 'wise up', it is to the Lord that we must we go. The prophetic charge to Israel to measure the claims of mediums and spiritists against God's Word (Isa. 8:19-20) applies not only to our contemporary critique of modern spiritualists and New Age adepts, but also to our response to the conventional wisdom that presently dominates in our culture; that is to say, we must examine, in the light of God's Word, the prevailing scientistic, materialistic humanism that admits no absolutes, no principles, no insights, and no facts outside of the senses and intelligence of autonomous man.

Why do we need wisdom? (7:15)

Solomon's answer is that the world is downside up! The early Christians were dragged before the authorities with the complaint that they had 'turned the world upside down' (Acts 17:6). Unbelievers recognized that the gospel offered a radical challenge to the *status quo*. Christ came to a world in which the down side was up. Through the witness of his church, he means to reverse that 180 degrees, by bringing people and societies from the dominion of darkness to the kingdom of the Son the Father loves, through redemption and the forgiveness of sins (Col. 1:13).

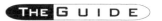

WHAT THE TEXT TEACHES

The trouble is that the down side still seems very much in the ascendant, even after two thousand years of the preaching of the gospel of Christ. The Preacher observes the disconcerting realities: 'a just man who perishes in his righteousness', and 'a wicked man who prolongs his life in his wickedness' (7:15). Echoes of the psalmist's reflections are heard here. He saw, in his time, 'the wicked in great power, and spreading himself like a native green tree' (Ps. 37:35).

1. Does evil prove God is powerless and uncaring?

At first, this gave the Psalmist some problems. 'When I thought how to understand this, it was too painful for me' (Ps. 73:16). What a perfectly understandable response! Paradoxes are bound to pose a problem, because they are, *ipso facto*, grey contradictions of somebody's cherished black-and-white assumptions. We like things to be cut and dried, either ... or, black and white. It is tidy, clean, even logical. This is good and that is wrong, is much more appealing than the ethical murkiness of grey and fuzzy assessments of probabilities and possibilities. We like simple answers. They are, on the face of it, more convenient. But is that always the case? Suppose we say, 'God is good, therefore he will instantly crush evil!' We are all well aware that there is plenty of evil about and it is not showing signs of dying out! Some use that observation to argue that either God isn't good enough to care or just isn't there at all. Less radically, many Christians feel confused, as did the psalmist, because God does not seem to intervene with the alacrity we feel he ought to.

2. A plan of salvation takes time

But does it really follow from the doctrine of the goodness of God that he should instantly and for ever banish all evil and turn this world into the perfection of heaven?

Does this notion hold water? The more he thought about it, the psalmist was convinced that it didn't. He found the answer in what, to modern ears, must seem an unlikely place — 'the sanctuary of God', i.e. the temple (Ps. 73:17). There he was faced with the fact that God *is* and that he has a *plan of redemption* for lost sinners in a perishing world. This resolved — and still resolves — the paradox of a down-side-up world. Why? Because everything about the temple preached God's covenantal commitment to save a people for himself out of *successive generations* of people.[4] This obviously involved time — time during which God would call the nations to repent and believe, time in which redemption in Christ would 'spread through the many' (i.e. to more and more people), and 'from sea to sea' and 'to the ends of the earth' (2 Cor. 4:15; Ps. 72:8), and, just as clearly, time for the judgements of God to be applied throughout the same generations (Ps. 73:17-20).

God is dealing with us as individuals, generation after generation. And the context of his redemptive work is a sin-wracked world in which
he calls people to look to him and be saved.
When the psalmist — in this case Asaph — was
gripped by this truth, his heart was stilled, he
rejoiced in God his Saviour, and he committed
himself to witness to his sovereign Lord: 'l will
declare all your works' (Ps. 73:28; cf. vv. 23-
28).

3. God's wisdom makes the difference

How did everything in the real world — in particular, the paradox of the wicked prospering and
the righteous suffering — come together for the
psalmist? Through wisdom from God! Only in
terms of the light of God's revelation could he
make sense of it all. In the light of God's purpose
of salvation the real world was intelligible. He
was then able to discern the hand of God at work.
And this is the precise point the Preacher is concerned to get across in the rest of the chapter. It
takes spiritual wisdom, born of the Spirit of God
and informed by the Word of God, to see the
world in a balanced perspective and not be
unhinged by the often hideous realities that
thrust themselves upon the lives of people and
societies. Wising up to God's wisdom is the burden of our Scripture passage.

WHAT THE TEXT TEACHES

How do we get wisdom? (7:16-18)

Wisdom has been called 'the golden mean'.[5] The related idea in the field of personal behaviour is that of 'moderation in all things'. Today we perhaps find this language rather musty. It seems to suggest that the Christian should never take strong and decisive positions. He should be decisively nice and avoid being even slightly dogmatic. By and large, this has indeed been the dominant ethos of mainstream Christianity, certainly with respect to personal ethics. The effect has been to reduce the claims of the Christian faith from a programme of radical life-transforming discipleship to Christ to a kind of lace-curtain gentility expressing the prevailing norms of middle-class culture. This is relevant to our understanding of what the Preacher has to tell us about avoiding extremes (7:18), because, if there is one thing that he cannot be accused of, it is being nice and nonconfrontational or undecided in his views. The Preacher is strong medicine. He does not mince words. And when he talks about avoiding extremes, he is focusing on specific exaggerated sins. He is not advocating a mealy-mouthed moderatism, in which doctrinal and ethical uncertainty is made a virtue and definite, scripturally formed views are dismissed as extreme, immature and unloving.

God's way is portrayed as being in the centre of the picture. It is a way of truth and of divine love for those who walk in it. It is very clearly defined and allows no confusion or evasion. Jesus calls it the 'narrow' road

(Matt. 7:14). This is the measure of what is extreme. And what the Preacher here warns against as extreme are paths that deviate from God's path, whether to the right or to the left. Holy moderation is the avoidance of sin; sin is the measure of what is extreme.

What, then, are the guidelines for beginning to be wise? The writer points out three things: two are cautions and the third a positive and fundamental basis for growth.

1. Don't deceive yourself (7:16)

Becoming self-righteous or imagining yourself to be an intellectual giant is not the same as true wisdom, but evidence of a destructive self-centredness (7:16). The language is ironic. The charge not to be 'overrighteous' or 'overwise' cannot be a proscription of either personal holiness or the possession of great wisdom. Rather, hypocritical pretension and self-deceit are in view. It is very easy for people to make a show of what they think is their goodness, and for clever people to parade what they think is their wisdom. The only corrective is the Holy Spirit-given, born-again humility that gives us a true view of who we are before God (Rom. 7:18). Then there will be more humble working faith and less playing at religion, more of the heart and less of the externals, more of God and less of self. The first extreme to avoid is that of self-righteousness.

2. Don't indulge yourself (7:17)

The second caution is very startling: 'Do not be *overly* wicked' (7:17). This seems to suggest the possibility that moderate wickedness can be part of a good and balanced life! Yet we know from Scripture that God will not look upon sin and that to be guilty of one point of his law is to be guilty of it all (Hab. 1:13; James 2:10). With God, *any* wickedness is too much wickedness. We are called to be perfect as he is perfect (1 Peter 1:16). How then can we square the Preacher with all this bedrock truth? Is he not saying exactly what the world wants to believe: Sow your wild oats, cheat a little here and there, but don't go over the top?

The answer is surely that he is saying there is enough wickedness clinging to our souls without giving ourselves over to it! The context is a discussion of wisdom. Would it be wise to indulge sin? The answer? 'Why should you die before your time?' (7:17). That extreme is no nearer to wisdom and blessing than the path of the self-righteous.

3. Fear God! (7:18)

The founders of my *alma mater*, the University of Aberdeen, gave it the motto, *Initium sapientiae timor Domini* — drawn from Psalm 111:10; Proverbs 1:7 and 9:10. Wisdom begins with the fear of God (7:18). Why? Because the fear of God — a reverent and personal submission to the Lord and his revealed will in his Word — rests in his definition of what is righteous and what is sinful and so avoids the pitfalls of legalism on the one hand and antinomianism (the belief that Christians are free from observing the moral law, due to grace) on the other.

Speaking of these pitfalls of carnal pseudo-righteousness and just plain carnality, Solomon points out that, 'It is good that you grasp this, and also not remove your hand from the other' (7:18). In other words, grasp the dangers of self-righteousness and never let go of your convictions about the sinfulness of sin. Significantly, this is the same language used by Jesus in his awesome condemnation of the Pharisees, recorded in Matthew's Gospel. Referring to their attention to tiny details of ritual righteousness and their gross unrighteousness with respect to the central principles of God's law, the Lord said to them, 'These you ought to have done, without leaving the others undone' (Matt. 23:23). Jesus shows that excessive righteousness and excessive wickedness are really two extremes that come together in the same people. The former is a cover for the latter.

But the true fear of God leads away from such things. This is not the naked terror of swift and terrible punishment by a barely known deity poised ready to crush the slightest slip. It is the holy — and loving — fear of the child for a father he knows loves him. It is the reverence that realizes that his heavenly Father has a purpose of

grace for him and has set before him the way of life
and joy in the fellowship of faith in his Saviour Lord.

QUESTIONS FOR DISCUSSION

1. Do you think it's true that 'people may run away from
   problems but problems never run away from people'?
   Why don't evasion, escapism, emigration and eremitism
   (becoming a hermit) work?

2. Why does God think wisdom is relevant to our life
   experience?

3. How and why is this world downside up (v.15; Ps.
   37:35)? How does God challenge this situation (Acts
   17:6)? In Psalm 73:16-28 what made David revise his
   estimation of the prosperity of the wicked?

4. Why are we warned about being excessively righteous,
   wise and wicked (7:16-17)? Does this mean we can be
   moderately foolish and sinful (1 Peter 1:16)? How does
   true wisdom avoid extremes (7:18; Prov. 1:7)?

CHAPTER SIXTEEN

WISING UP

BIBLE READING

Ecclesiastes 7:19 - 8:1

If we begin with the fear of God, we will continue with an honest appraisal of our personal weakness. We will be ready to be vulnerable before God, men and ourselves. 'Vulnerability' is very much in vogue in contemporary culture, but it is more focused on securing the sympathy and indulgence of others that it is on learning and changing destructive patterns of thought and behaviour. It is one thing to cry about your failings. It is quite something else to commit yourself in your weakness to God's programme for renewal and reformation. Vulnerability without the fear of God will never rise very far above self-pity and, perhaps, a desire to somehow fulfil one's own potential, whatever that may mean in practice. If you will not look up to the Lord, you are bound to look in to yourself. If you do look to the Lord, then there are a number of practical implications for the way in which you will think about your problems and, not least, where you will expect to find the solutions. In this passage, Solomon leads us from the *starting point* (7:19-

22), through the *journey* (7:23-29), and on to the *goal* of becoming truly wise in heart (8:1).

Starting point: admitting your need (7:19-22)

We must first recognize *the real strength of wisdom* — it makes one wise man more powerful than 'ten rulers of the city' (7:19). The wisdom of God is the rightness of God. That is strength. The number and position of those who oppose it only tells us how easy it is for us to be fools.

We must also recognize *our need of wisdom*. Even the best of people are flawed (7:20). Everyone sins. Weakness is in our nature. We need that powerful input from outside of ourselves which only the wisdom of God can provide. We must, therefore, admit our personal weakness.

This implies that we must *act wisely and generously* with respect to the faults of others. Otherwise there will be no end of disquiet and strife. For example, what people say is often unhelpful, if not injurious. It is better not to know everything that people say (7:21-22; James 3:2). You may hear more than you want to hear, more than you need to hear. And if you hear your servant cursing you, you should remember that 'many times also … you have cursed others' (7:22). Learn from the hurtful things you have said of others. How much good did they achieve? What good will it do to hear similar things said of yourself?

Solomon mentions this to show that wisdom acts like an editor of life's experiences. It selects what is helpful and trashes in advance what would have harmful effects. Like a good editor, wisdom does not chase the wrong story. It does not eavesdrop. It does not listen in the wrong places. It slanders no one, but is 'peaceable, gentle, showing all humility toward all men' (Titus 3:2).

Journey: working at wisdom (7:23-29)

Given a basic faith-commitment (the fear of God) and a vulnerable attitude, how may one grow in wisdom? Solomon gives four lines of approach that will lead to a deepening understanding of what is happening in our lives.

1. Understand your own limitations (7:23-24)

Solomon had given a great deal of thought to the meaning of life. He had been determined to be wise and had 'proved [i.e. tested] by wisdom' all sorts of problems and solutions — that is, everything discussed thus far in Ecclesiastes (7:23). The deeper you sink, the sooner you hit the bottom. 'But this was far from me' denotes his unconditional surrender to human finitude and frailty. The human brain is a powerful weapon in the quest for understanding, but even at the level of marshalling simple facts, it is very limited. It was all beyond him. In our world, the body of knowledge is so vast that the days of the polymath — a brilliant individual, like a Leonardo da Vinci or an Isaac Newton, with an almost comprehensive knowledge of a wide range of subjects — is gone for ever. Wisdom has always been more elusive than mere knowledge of facts about the world. Wisdom touches eternity and the mind of God. Bowing before the very concept of God's omniscience (his complete knowledge of everything), the psalmist declares, 'Such knowledge is too wonderful for me; it is high, I cannot attain it' (Ps. 139:6).

Charles Bridges is so right when he says that 'our highest knowledge is but a mere atom, when compared with the unsearchable extent of our ignorance. The more we know of God — his nature (Job 9:7) — his works (Psalm 92:5) — his dispensations (Romans 11:33), the more we are humbled in the sense of our ignorance'.[1] This is what Augustine called '*docta ignorantia*' — informed or learned ignorance[2] — the kind of knowledge that is content with its real limitations and able with a quiet spirit to trust a loving Father-God for all that we cannot know.

2. Understand the human problem (7:25)

Again he applies his mind to the human condition. The words 'applied', 'heart', 'to know', 'to search', 'seek out', 'wisdom', 'the reason of things', 'folly', 'wickedness', 'madness' and 'foolishness' together portray all the

Discipleship and wisdom

R.C.Sproul notes that 'The New Testament word for "disciple" means literally "a learner". The Christian is called to be enrolled in the school of Christ. Careful study of the Bible is necessary for true discipleship... A disciple does not dabble in learning. He makes the seeking after an understanding of God's Word a chief business of his life.'*

Most Christians hardly read their Bibles and never read a good Christian book. Mention 'doctrine' and their eyes glaze over. And these are often the same people who are well educated and possess great talents. They would never dream of being as sloppy in their thinking in their regular work and study, as they are when it comes to the Bible and Christian discipleship. They seem to think that ignorance of the Bible and sound teaching is no hindrance to discipleship.

Knowledge and wisdom are two different things. Of course, you cannot have the one without the other. Knowledge grows into wisdom, when it is tempered by love for the Lord and applied by the Holy Spirit in a renewed heart and mind. What are you doing to cultivate the wisdom which alone will make you grow in discipleship to Jesus? A ten-minute 'quiet time'? Hearing a 15-20 minute sermon in church once a week? Attendance at Bible study group once in a while? That kind of 'commitment' would never get you through a basic course of study anywhere in the world. It would never be enough to keep a job that required any kind of expertise. Worldly people know what it takes to get ahead in their world. Many Christians seem to think that God will be happy with mediocrity and lack of diligence in his disciples. Is it time to change your ways?

* R.C. Sproul, *In the Presence of God*
(Nashville: Word, 1999), p. 136.

intensity of a great intellect striving to make sense of a profound enigma. It is precisely the stark contrasts in human behaviour that pose the conundrum. How can rational man be so irrational? Why does the image-bearer of God sometimes stoop to the most brutalizing and dehumanizing excesses? Why is a world so full of life disfigured by so much misery and death? And why, more personally, have I found this out not just by reading the newspapers and keeping my eyes open, but by doing it myself — by experimenting with foolishness and self-destructive wickedness? Solomon calls us to reflect upon what we do and why we do it. And we are to measure it against the wisdom that begins with the fear of God (7:18).

3. Understand relationships (7:26-28)

The central strand that runs through the human condition is the sin factor with 'its certain tendency to our misery and ruin'.[3] Because none of us is an island, this expresses itself in our relationships. Solomon finds sexual relationships that have gone wrong the most bitter of all. In particular, he warns against the predatory seductress who will surely ensnare the sinner and from whom only 'he who pleases God' will 'escape' (7:26). Given our modern sensitivities to sexist language, it is important to set these words in their proper context. Solomon is speaking here from personal experience and he speaks as a man. He was certainly no woman hater (cf. 9:9). He is not saying that men are not guilty of their own brand of predacious misdemeanours toward women. His observations are simply from his personal viewpoint. And it is significant that he realizes his own need of God's power to keep him from sin. He does not blame the temptress for his own weaknesses. Like Paul, he saw the need of God-centred self-control (1 Cor. 9:7). And in the area of sex, this is all the more essential because of the power of the emotions involved and the potential for harmful effects on individual, family and community life. Broken relationships are often broken from the start, just because those entering into them do so without any solid basis. When Solomon later talks about the joy of happy marriage, he clearly sees that arising from a mutual commitment to marriage as God has planned it — a monogamous, lifelong relationship for partnership, procreation and, not least, piety.

In assessing men and women in general, he finds very little to encourage him. His poetic statistics for the relative uprightness of men and women cannot be meant to draw any serious comparison between the two. To suggest, as he does, that men are one-tenth of one per cent better than women is to deride the very idea! It is equivalent to saying, with the psalmist, 'There is none who does good, no, not one' (Ps. 14:3; cf. Rom. 3:10-12). Like Diogenes, Solomon is looking for an honest person, and he is looking in vain. It is a sober comment on man's need of salvation.

4. Understand God's plan (7:29)

While the writer's conclusion is that mankind has only itself to blame for its predicament ('but they have sought out many schemes'), the truth is that God made us for something better ('God made man upright', 7:29). Almost cryptically, he hints at a redemptive purpose in God's mind. Why else would he be writing? Is the only reason for mentioning that God made man upright at the beginning to exonerate God from responsibility for man's subsequent regression? Surely not! There is hope, and it is rooted in God's plan for the human race. What does God have in store? Look to him! Listen to his voice! Turn to him in obedience! Please him and serve him! Wise up with the wisdom that God is revealing to his people!

The goal: the truly wise man (8:1)

Wise people are a treasure. 'Who is like a wise man?' (8:1). Wise people are distinguished by a depth of knowledge and understanding of life and its meaning and purpose. They know 'the interpretation of a thing'. But this is no mere head knowledge. It is light that shines from the innermost being. The Lord says he 'will beautify the meek with salvation' (Ps. 149:4, AV). True wisdom passes a very practical test: 'A man's wisdom makes his face shine, and the sternness of his face is changed' (8:1). That brightness is the light of Christ's righteousness shining forth in a life of practical

godliness. Knowing the Lord softens facial fea-
tures as much as it melts the hardness of the
heart. The Christian is a letter to the world,
'known and read by all men' (2 Cor. 3:2). Christ,
who is the wisdom of God, is read on the faces
of those who love him (1 Cor. 1:24). Wise up ...
in Christ your personally embraced Saviour!
Then let your light shine brightly that they may
see your good deeds and come to praise your
Father in heaven.

QUESTIONS FOR DISCUSSION

1. *Why is being vulnerable before God, others, and ourselves so much a part of gaining true wisdom (7:19-22)?*

2. *How can we grow in wisdom? Outline the four steps in 7:23-29.*

3. *Who is the wise man? How can we identify him (8:1)?*

DISCUSS IT

CHAPTER
SEVENTEEN

RESPECT
AUTHORITY!

LOOK IT UP

BIBLE READING

Ecclesiastes 8:2-8

INTRODUCTION

The father watched his three-year-old son run around the doctor's waiting room. The toddler paused only to slam the door open and shut … and again … and again. 'Don't do that, or the people in the office will spank you,' said his Dad (telling a lie). 'No they won't,' retorted the boy (calling his Dad's bluff). And on he went, slamming the door back and forth. 'Then I'll spank you,' came the weak reply (an idle threat, never acted upon). Turning to the receptionist, he lamented, in the hearing of his little whirling dervish, that the lad was 'too smart' for him. 'He's all right with other people, but with his Mom and Dad he's the first to tell them to "Go to hell!" He sure knows when you're [expletive deleted] him!' Then, having provided this foul-mouthed bad example and tacitly abdicated his parental responsibility, he managed to gather his little charge and steer him out of the office.

This story is an eyewitness account. It is being repeated in millions of families, and is symptomatic of the disintegration of the social fabric of the Western 'post-Christian' world. When we think of the breakdown of authority and order, we naturally associate it with crime and terrorism. We think of it in terms of law and order and the power or weakness of the judicial system of the State. The figures for the crime rate are routinely greeted with a plaintive litany about lenient judges, inadequate penalties, and too few policemen. The underlying assumption is that the State is weak and that all the woes of societal breakdown arise from this source. It is very questionable, however, whether the facts can sustain such a thesis.

The State is not weak in the sense that it is unwilling to employ severe measures to achieve its particular goals. It is not lenient where its own security is threatened. Treason and fraud against government agencies often draw more severe sentences than crimes against the person, including murder. What we are seeing is not leniency *per se* on the part of the judiciary, but a shift in perspectives and priorities in society as a whole. A transformation has taken place in the way in which authority and respect for authority are viewed in the West. Lawlessness and lenient sentences arise from a mass decline of the will to be law-abiding — the decline of that mainstay of stable societies, the law-abiding citizen. This represents the creeping anarchy that cannot but result from the rejection of the very idea of a law that has absolute standards of right and wrong. The three-year-old in the doctor's office has no respect for his father's authority because there is no true authority

to respect in his father. The father does not really know what law is and is therefore incapable of providing his child with any consistent system of order. He is actually teaching the child spiritual anarchy. When he does assert some control, it is by the violence of a foul mouth and occasional, even arbitrary, force. The essential point is that the basis, in terms of principles, for discerning right from wrong has eroded away.

From the Preacher's viewpoint, spiritual and ethical anarchism was but another aspect of the meaninglessness of under-the-sun secularized life. Where there is no God, absolutes cannot exist; relativism rules, and that means that people will do what they can get away with — and even define it as good. Yet, precisely because it is the ethics of shifting sand, injustice and frustration are its most prominent fruits. Therefore, in addressing the question as to how this meaninglessness can be rolled back, it is to be expected that God's Word would teach us that we can be happy and enjoy his blessing in a proper respect for authority, both civil and divine. Having told us that we can learn from experience (7:1-14) and grow in wisdom as God's children (7:15 - 8:1), it is a short step to bring us to the prospect of enjoying the good hand of God in the context of an ordered life (8:2-3). Two main themes attract the writer's attention in Ecclesiastes 8. The first theme is the positive principle that we are called, in the Lord, to be obedient to the civil authorities (8:2), and the second theme, the subject of a succeeding study, is that God will bless his people even under injustice and an oppressive government (8:12).

Obey the King (8:2-4)

At the beginning of every Cub or Scout meeting (at least we *did*, forty years ago) we held up our right hands in salute and recited the 'Cub's/Scout's Promise'. This included a solemn undertaking to 'do [our] duty to God and the Queen'. In all the years I was in the Scouting movement, I must have recited that promise hundreds of times, yet that central promise is all that I remember of it. It seemed to me then, as it still does, a very momentous pledge. It is not a profession of faith in Christ or a commitment to a denominational creed, but a politico-religious loyalty oath to the Crown — the monarch being the personification of the British Constitution. The Pledge of Allegiance in the United States enshrines a similar commitment, although in notably less direct language. The phrase 'one Nation under God' envisions the Almighty as more of a witness to the pledge than the object of the duties pledged, but he is nevertheless the paramount witness who, in some sense, is assumed to be sovereign over the nation, who has an interest in both the affairs of the nation and the sincerity of the allegiance being pledged.

Moral relativism

The Christian publisher and journalist, Russ Pulliam, writing in *The Indianapolis News,* comments on the astonishing fact that a high school newspaper in Ohio could run a series of articles on cheating without once indicating that cheating was wrong. 'The problem', says Pulliam, 'runs deeper than just adding values education to the curriculum or learning some standards of right and wrong. With a few notable exceptions, the world of learning is dominated by thinkers filled with doubts, not necessarily about the existence of God — but doubts about the certainty that God has revealed universal standards of right and wrong to all people. If God has not revealed such standards, then the efforts to teach ethics is doomed from the beginning. It's just one person's opinion against another's.'*

This is *moral relativism.* What it means in practice is that everyone does, or tries to do, what is right in his own eyes, and the result is lawless behaviour throughout every level of society (cf. Judges 17:6). Is this what you see in your world? Maybe even in the way you think and do things? How do people define 'right' and 'wrong' today? By absolute truth from God's revealed Word, the Bible? Or in relation to something like cultural acceptability, so-called 'community standards' or 'common sense'? Or no more than personal feelings?

Why, in the last analysis, must all alternatives to God's standards be man's self-invented values? How can they be anything other than self-serving, when inevitably they are tailored to suit the interests of those who promote them?

*Russ Pulliam, 'The Basis for Right and Wrong'
(*Covenanter Witness*, Vol. 123:12 (Dec. 1987).
Reprinted from *The Indianapolis News.*

1. Rulers are to be obeyed

This is precisely the import of the Preacher's first major proposition. It is that *rulers are to be obeyed*: 'Keep the king's commandment for the sake of your oath to God' (8:2). It seems that there was some kind of pledge of allegiance in ancient Israel. Whatever it was, it is clear that submission to the king was made by a solemn oath before God and it is equally clear that this was, and is, consistent with the teaching of the Word of God. We are, for example, to 'Fear God, [and] honour the king' (1 Peter 2:17). The Scriptures are explicit on this point. The *locus classicus* is, of course, Romans 13:1-5, where the central principle is laid down that 'the authorities that exist are appointed by God' (13:1). Because of this, 'you must be subject, not only because of wrath but also for conscience' sake' (13:5). The practical reason — the fear of punishment — is mentioned first, one supposes, because it is the one reason that always comes immediately to everyone's mind. No one ever wants to suffer the punishments of the law! The Preacher therefore urges a realistic respect and circumspection in dealing with the authorities. Even in obeying the law, it is wise to show respect for its majesty and power. Don't hurry away from the king's presence or stand up for a bad cause (8:3). Take account of the king's power and avoid provoking his displeasure unnecessarily (8:4).

2. Rulers are to desire to obey God

There is, however, a deeper, distinctly theological reason for a prudent and respectful submission to authority, namely a conscientious desire to obey God. This is the more profound reason because it gives expression to the true basis for all submission to the authorities. It is not, as we shall see, a case of blind unquestioning obedience of the 'my country right or wrong' variety. The oath implies that there is a higher allegiance due to God himself. His will is the first and most important consideration in this, as in all aspects of life. At the same time, situations can arise in which obeying God means disobeying the authorities (Acts 4:19; 5:29). There are things to be rendered to Caesar and other things to be rendered to God (Matt. 22:21). But Scripture is clear that within its proper, God-defined sphere, civil government is to be submitted to *out of a desire* to *follow* the *Lord faithfully.* The time may come, when, like the apostles, 'we obey God rather than men' (Acts 5:29, AV), but until that moment we are called by God to submit to the powers that be.

Knowing the proper time (8:5-7)

God-honouring submission to authority is never *blind* obedience. The State is neither our conscience nor our ultimate sovereign. We are never called by God to a blindly passive and amorally slavish conformity to whatever laws men may decide to impose. We are actually called to an active, analytical, and ethically biblical response, even in the face of potentially threatening consequences. If this is done with wisdom, the danger may be averted and it may even be possible to achieve great things. 'A wise man's heart discerns both time and judgment' (8:5); that is to say, he will know what to do, how to do it and when the time is ripe.

At the best of times this requires patience and an ability to read the signs. This came home to me in a brush with the police in Turkey. On an overnight train ride across Anatolia, we had dozed off for no more than half an hour and awoke to find our cameras had been stolen from the overhead luggage rack, where we had so foolishly hidden them in plain sight. When we arrived in Uskudar (the Scutari made famous by Florence Nightingale), on the Asian side of the Bosporus from Istanbul, we made a beeline for the police office at the train station. The policeman on duty evidently had us nondescript backpackers pegged as a pair of Western hippies. It was the mid-1960s, and we were two newly graduated zoologists on the way home from a field trip to the Taurus Mountains. He immediately accused us of selling the cameras, and refused to register our report — which we needed in order to recover the insurance back in Britain. My friend was a deal bolder than I: he didn't take it lying down. He sounded

off to that policeman as if the whole of the Royal Navy were off-shore with its guns trained on that little office! But the more he protested, the surlier that policeman became. We realized our tactical error and quietly withdrew to the British consulate. Only when a consular official took us to the central police station in Istanbul were we able to come away with the paper we needed.

There is a proper time and correct procedure! There are numerous examples of this in the Bible. Jonathan, for example, chose exactly the right moment to speak to his father Saul about David (1 Sam. 19:4-6). Nathan the prophet told David a story about a stolen lamb and then, with impeccable timing, rebuked David for stealing another man's wife (2 Sam. 12:1-14). Esther went in to King Ahasuerus in such a way as to effect the salvation of the entire Jewish community in the Persian Empire (Esther 7:2-4).

But why is there a proper 'time and judgment' for every matter (8:6)? The Preacher's answer is — and it sounds strange to begin with — that no one knows the future (8:7). Why does he say this? Because not knowing the future makes us frustrated — 'the misery of man increases greatly', or, as the NIV has it, 'weighs heavily upon him' (8:6). In turn, being frustrated causes us to rush in where angels fear to tread! Impatience always tends to make a mess of things. There is only one answer to this problem. Jesus gave it to the disciples when he sent them out to evangelize the Jews: 'But when they deliver you up, do not worry about how or what you should speak. For it will be given to you in that hour what you should speak; for it is not you who speak, but the Spirit of your Father who speaks in you' (Matt. 10:19-20). This is a promise for all believers. The Holy Spirit will lead his people and instruct them in the spirit of their minds. The right time and procedure will be made plain to those who truly seek the Lord's will with a patient and trusting attitude.

The limits of human authority (8:8)

God-honouring submission to authority does not imply *unlimited* obedience. The Preacher has spoken of the propriety of obedience toward our rulers (8:2). He also spoke of the importance of careful procedure in approaching the authorities, especially when some change is desired (8:5-7). Now, just in case we feel that we have no freedom of thought or action in relation to the power of the State, he tells us that it has very real limitations. However wise and respectful we ought to be to kings and politicians, we need not be cowed into servility or craven fear in their presence. They do not have unlimited power. The State is not God, however totalitarian its aspirations and policies may be, however godlike its pretensions to regulate the lives of its subjects. These limits are evident in two monolithic facts.

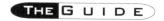

WHAT THE TEXT TEACHES

1. God reserves some powers (8:8)

'No one has power over the spirit to retain the spirit' (8:8). The Hebrew here is *ruah* which sometimes means 'wind' (thus NIV), but in this context is properly to be rendered 'spirit'.[1] The human spirit is beyond the control of human authority. Likewise, 'no one has power in the day of death' (8:8). 'Ah,' you say, 'but kings and dictators have exercised power over the day of the deaths of millions of their victims!' True, but what the Preacher is getting at is that human authority cannot *prevent* death when that day has come. The day of each person's death proves the limit of human power. When King Canute set his throne before the rising tide and thereby demonstrated that he could not hold back the ocean's waves, he proved, dramatically and, contrary to legend, quite deliberately, that he was not to be regarded by his subjects as possessing godlike powers.[2] Is the human spirit any easier to contain than the wind and the waves? Can the power of government prevent minds from thinking their own thoughts? The fact is that the tentacles of the greatest tyrannies have failed to crush the life out of the human spirit, far less thwart the purposes of God. And what of all the confidence that emanates from the corridors of power? And the apparently limitless pretensions of politicians to better the lot of mankind and control human destiny? Who remembers the Locarno Pact between the Great Powers that, in 1925, forever abolished war as a means of solving disputes between nations? Did seventy years of official atheism under communism remove Christianity from the face of Russia? The events of human history are ordered by the Lord 'that the nations may know themselves to be but men' (Ps. 9:20).

2. *God exercises his judgement (8:8)*

'Wickedness will not deliver those who are given to it' (8:8). This is as certain as the fact that 'no one is discharged in time of war' (8:8, NIV). The illustration is apt, for it is God, the avenger of wickedness and injustice, who wages war on those who oppress his people. The Preacher's point is that wickedness — the absolute power that corrupts absolutely — may seem to provide the despotic government with the means to impose its will limitlessly and to offer that government release from the problems it faces. Think of the draconian measures employed in Hitler's 'final solution' of the 'Jewish problem'. Ponder Stalin's slaughter of millions of property-owning peasants, the 'kulaks' and Pol Pot's destruction of a third of the entire nation of Cambodia/Kampuchea in the name of redemption from capitalist imperialism! And what did the self-styled 'king of Africa', Idi Amin Dada, achieve for Uganda by all his brutality but the transformation of the 'pearl of Africa', to use Winston Churchill's phrase, into a charnel-house? Unrestrained power collapses under its own weight. Evil destroys and self-destructs at one and the same time. But more than that, as E. W. Hengstenberg observes, such apparently irresistible powers 'have only importance until God's time and judgement draw nigh'.[3] God's power in the exercise of his righteous judgement (3:17) is the ultimate limitation of the ambitions of political power.

DISCUSS IT

QUESTIONS FOR DISCUSSION

1. *Why are we to respect the proper authorities (8:2-4; see also 1 Peter 2:17; Rom. 13:1-5)? Identify the **practical** and the **theological** reasons. Should we ever disobey the authorities?*

2. *Is this an unquestioning and unvarying obedience (8:5-7; see also Acts 4:19; 5:29; Matt. 22:21)? What does the Preacher mean by the proper 'time and judgment' (8:6)?*

3. *Are there limits to human authority (8:8)?*

CHAPTER
EIGHTEEN

COPING WITH INJUSTICE

BIBLE READING

Ecclesiastes 8:9-17

It is not always easy to respect authority. Abuse of authority is the rule in most of the modern world and at every level, global to local. Even in nations blessed with the checks and balances of a long tradition of personal freedom and the rule of law, injustice is rife, and the oppressed wage constant battle against those who simply want to take advantage of them. The Preacher's concern is with the proper response of faith to such a situation. How ought we to respond to the abuse of power and the injustice that follows in its train?

Injustice is rife (8:9-12,14)

The Preacher highlights five instances of injustice:

1. Authority is often exercised to the hurt of those whom it is supposed to serve (8:9). The RSV 'to

his hurt' is to be preferred to the AV/NIV/NKJV rendering 'to his own hurt'.[1] Self-destruction is not in view — the Preacher is thinking of the victims. To those at the receiving end, it is always painful to see a trust abused and those in authority become an enemy rather than a protector. This tests our faith, because it leads us to wonder why the Lord allows it all to happen.

2. The wicked are praised in life and eulogized in death in the very cities where they practised their injustices (8:10). It is one thing to observe the terms of the ancient maxim, *De mortuis nil nisi bonum* ('Say nothing but what is good of the dead'), but quite another to canonize an utter reprobate as if he were as pure as the driven snow! Injustice at this level also tests faith and tempts us to think that there may be no justice in the universe after all.

3. The sluggish execution of justice is observed to have the effect of encouraging lawlessness in others, as they become persuaded that they may get away with light punishment ... or even get away scot-free (8:11)! Justice deferred can seem like justice denied for ever.

4. The wicked are seen enjoying the benefits of their misdeeds throughout long lives, in the course of which they apparently avoid any penalty for their actions (8:12). It is almost becoming the custom nowadays for convicted criminals to write best-sellers about their wicked lives. This, too, seems manifestly unjust.

5. Often we see a reversal of natural justice — 'just men to whom it happens according to tho work of the wicked; again there are wicked men to whom it happens according to the work of the righteous' (8:14). We sometimes see startling examples of this — none more shocking than the Jews' rejection of Jesus and choice of Barabbas (John 18:40). But more frequently, perhaps, it is an undertone — like the background wash of a water-colour painting — a general feature of injustices great and small. Perhaps the only surprising thing about these phenomena is that they were recorded of a society that existed some 2,500 years ago! It takes no imagination to identify similar things going on today. Most of us could illustrate each point from the daily newspaper or even from the lives of people we know. There really is nothing new under the sun! And isn't it intriguing that the abuses the Preacher pinpoints are grassroot injustices — not the epic evils like mass murder, wars of aggression, and multi-million dollar stock-exchange frauds? It is not that the spectacular inhumanities of man to man are of lesser account — just that many of us are only touched by them through history books and the media. For the most part, it is the local injustices that materially affect us and wreak their havoc in our *real* world. Frustration with that neighbour who seems to will his dog to foul everyone's lawn but his own; resentment at a

local business that first conceals and then defends waste disposal practices that polluted the water supply; anger at the irresponsibility that siphons off tax money into politically motivated projects, while the roads decay and the truly needy are neglected. A climate of oppression can exist because of the 'little' things. And it is because these are such ever-present realities in a community or a nation that everything can seem to be meaningless (cf. 8:10,14).

Faith has an answer (8:12-13,15)

To man's universal experience of injustice, as exemplified in the above five instances, the Preacher offers two practical and God-centred answers. These are the answers of faith and are as universal in their applicability as the injustices he mentions are in their capacity to frustrate us.

Firstly, *the doctrine*. Consider the *destiny* of *the righteous and the wicked* (8:12-13). In an echo of Psalm 73, the Preacher affirms as an article of faith that the prosperity of the wicked is an illusion. Things will not ultimately go well for them, whatever appearances there may be to the contrary. On the other hand, he can say, 'I surely know that it will be well with those who fear God, who fear before him' (8:12). He *knows* in the sense that he believes with unshakeable faith. It is not what he has seen with his eyes in the world. It is what he sees with the eyes of faith — faith in what God has

THINK ABOUT IT

THINK ABOUT IT

Why be a believer, when unbelievers seem to get on fine?

Edward Reynolds (1593-1676), Bishop of Norwich, comments on Ecclesiastes 8:11: 'The prosperity of wicked men doth exceedingly strengthen and harden them in their wickedness … they go on securely, abusing the goodness and longsuffering of God unto presumption, which should have led them unto repentance (Rom. 2:4).'* The effect of this on believers can test their faith to the depths. Psalm 73 shows a believer (Asaph) discouraged and angry because the wicked seem to succeed in life far better than God's people. He was 'envious of the boastful' when he saw their prosperity. 'Surely I have cleansed my heart in vain,' he complains (Ps. 73:3,13).

1. How does he settle the matter in his own mind? Does he keep on moaning and give up his faith? (Ps. 73:17-20).

2. What commitments and outlook does he end up with? (Ps. 73:23-28).

3. Will you go to Ecclesiastes 8 and Psalm 73 whenever you are tempted to feel that your faith is costing you too much in the world?

* Edward Reynolds, *Whole Works*
(Morgan, PA, Soli Deo Gloria: 1998), Vol. IV, p. 178
(A Commentary on the Book of Ecclesiastes).

revealed, reinforced by his personal experience of God's grace. It is in the nature of faith to look beyond the evidence of the senses. 'Now faith is the substance of things hoped for, the evidence of things not seen' (Heb. 11:1). By faith, the believer knows that God's perfect justice is being worked out. And it is because of his faith in the doctrine of divine justice and the essential goodness of God that he can retain a sense of proportion about the as yet unredressed injustices of wicked people. To know the self-revealing God is to know that his will is being done and that this must end in the blessing of God's people and the overthrow of injustice and oppression and every other contradiction of the mind and will of God.

Secondly, *the practice follows from the doctrine*. The God who is just and good wants his people to *enjoy his good* gifts (8:15). God has *given*. This is the bedrock truth that is to motivate our use of all our gifts. Eat and drink and be glad! Don't let the perplexities of life poison your God-honouring enjoyment of all he has given you in life! 'For every creature of God is good,' says Paul, 'and nothing is to be refused if it is received with thanksgiving; for it is sanctified by the word of God and prayer' (1 Tim. 4:4-5). Christians should not only be the happiest people in the world, they should be *seen* to be enjoying the good gifts of God! The Christian life is often portrayed as a sad, narrow, restricted and joyless existence. A world that finds its joys in the pleasures of sin will always want to see it that way, but sometimes we Christians can give the impression of

an austere and brooding discontent with life. Perhaps we think it is more pious to be grieved all the time about the state of the world. Or maybe we take a perverse joy in constantly carping about other people's sins. Yet God is clear in wanting the leading motif of our lives to be a redeemed joy, relaxing in the sunshine of his smile and exulting in the assurance of his love. The Christian life is a festival, and like any celebration it is to be filled with joyous exhilaration (1 Cor. 5:8)!

The enigma remains (8:16-17)

These answers cannot begin to satisfy under-the-sun secularism. The under-the-sun philosophy has no God who brings the wicked to justice and rewards the faithfulness of the righteous. It therefore cannot find any great contentment while perceived grievances go without redress in this life.

This perhaps explains why we live in a society characterized by an obsessive commitment to litigation and multi-million-dollar claims against the slenderest of offences. It also suggests why, in societies less fertile for such legal manoeuvres, the frequently preferred option is that of revolution and the gun. Men without God must have it all now, or it will be gone for ever.

In contrast, God's people know by faith that they already have what really counts and will really last. They have it right now in their hearts. They see that there can be no ultimate answers in under-the-sun terms, no perfect world through man's best efforts, no fully satisfactory resolution of injustice outside the complete outworking of God's eternal plans and purposes. It would be dishonest for any Christian to say that he is not troubled by the fact that his Father-God continues, generation after generation, to permit bad things to happen in the world. To trust that God will sort everything out in the end, in his own good time, is a comfort, but it does not remove the heart-cry for an end to sorrow and tears (see Rev. 6:9-11). To enjoy the good things that God has given does not cancel out the painful anomalies and inequities so obvious in the global condition of humankind. The enigma remains: even God's people know his blessing and his grace in tension with their as yet unfulfilled desire for the completion of his work of redemption and the full establishment of the final kingdom of Christ.

However much we understand, writes Charles Bridges, 'a vast *terra incognita* lies beyond us'.[2] The work of understanding must not stop, but the wisdom and knowledge of God is a great deep (Rom. 11:33). It is said that the first lesson taught by the Greek philosopher-mathematician Pythagoras was silence.[3] This was surely a wise echo of the foundational claim of the living God: 'Be still, and know that I am God' (Ps. 46:10). The Preacher expresses the paradox of faith: 'Then I saw all the work of God, that a man cannot find out the work that is done under the sun' (8:17). He saw all and consequently could not comprehend all. The more he learned, the less he grasped. He bowed in awe before the all-knowing God in realization of his utter dependence upon his Saviour!

QUESTIONS FOR DISCUSSION

1. What injustices do people often have to face (8:9-15)? Discuss the writer's five examples and his suggestions as to how we may cope with them.

2. Will we ever fully understand what is going on (8:16-I7)?

3. What is the relevance of faith to the enigmas of life (Heb. 11:1; Rom. 11:33; Ps. 46:10)?

DISCUSS IT

CHAPTER
NINETEEN

IS THERE ANY HOPE?

BIBLE READING

Ecclesiastes 9:1-6

'Things go better with Coke,' claims the famous Coca-Cola advertisement. Whatever the intrinsic merit of the product, there is one undeniable truth behind this statement, and it is this: people are motivated to spend money in the belief that their purchases will bring them some tangible benefit. All advertising sells hope before we ever buy fulfilment. No one commits himself knowingly to something that has no reward of some kind somewhere along the road. This is a fact of life.

We can all understand this in the world of consumer economics. But is this true of spiritual — specifically, Christian — commitment? Is it perhaps rather crass to think of Christian faith and life in terms of rewards? I think of a prayer I heard frequently at school assemblies in my youth.[1] The central line of thought was that the Christian's reward was in knowing he was doing God's will. We were 'to minister and not to be ministered unto; to labour and not to seek for any reward, save that of knowing that we do Thy Will'. This sounds so terribly noble and impregnably spiritual. Not for us the earthly returns of the stock market or the bounty hunter; ours is the inward satisfaction of a job well done for God! On reflection, however, this has to beg some questions. What is the place of hope and reward in the Christian life? Do we look only for inner peace arising from the assurance that we are doing God's will? Is the Christian faith an exclusively existential experience, as implied in the prayer? Does it have tangible rewards now and hereafter? Is a life of Christian hope only a trip — or does it lead somewhere real, eternal and heavenly?

A young Christian — in his second year in university — was talking one day with some Christian friends. 'You know,' he said, 'when I think about the Christian life... Well, supposing we die and there actually is nothing in it ... no heaven, no eternal life, no God even ... I think it would still be worth living ... it is a *better* way to live ... a happier, cleaner, more useful way... Don't you think?' One fellow shook his head, 'Man, if there is really nothing in the Christian faith, nothing in the promises of God, then we'd be fools for believing a lie! Why would we bother ourselves with it all? If there is really no God, no heaven, no salvation ... just death and the end ... then you might convince yourself the "Christian life" is nice and makes you happy, but don't pretend that that means anything. You might as well live a life of sin because it would be all the same in the end. It would all be a lie! It is because the promises of

God *are* true and because we actually do have a *destiny* in time and eternity in Christ, that our lives have meaning and purpose. We are going somewhere. And we know where we are going because Christ has told us, he leads us, and he will ever be with us until the day he gathers all his people together in glory!' His point was that a 'this world only' faith, however happy it may feel, is all journey and no destination, and hence no more than an illusion.

This, it so happens, is exactly the New Testament view of the subject: 'If in this life only we have hope in Christ, we are of all men the most pitiable' (1 Cor. 15:19). Paul's point is that because Christ actually, bodily rose from the dead, then in him all believers have an eternal destiny of resurrection life in glory. If our hope is a mere fantasy to be lived out in this world only, we are pathetic, pitiful people!

But even the assertion of a sure and certain hope of heaven calls forth the criticism that all we really have is 'pie in the sky, by and by'. It may be real, but it is not yet ours. Meanwhile, what use is being a believer here and now? What is God doing for us in this world, if indeed he is so all-powerful as to secure our future in the next? The negative, even mocking, tendency of this line of questioning is painfully obvious. It is in the same vein as that which Christ had to endure as he hung on the cross; 'If you are the King of the Jews, save yourself' (Luke 23:37). A

God who has prepared a heaven for his people ought to be seen to be doing them some good on the earth!

This argument may beg some questions, but it strikes an uneasy note in many a believer's heart. It is a fair question. Why do God's people not live out their lives in a glowing corona of success and consistent holiness? The fact is — and the Preacher saw this in his day — that when it comes to the normal run of life, the righteous and the wicked have much the same experience. And sometimes injustices are visited on the righteous, while the wicked get on pretty well (cf. 8:14). What then are the advantages, if any, in being a child of God in this world?

The paradox of providence (9:1)

Before answering this, the Preacher muses on an essential paradox of the believer's life: 'For I considered all this in my heart, so that I could declare it all: that the righteous and the wise and their works are in the hand of God. People know neither love nor hatred by anything they see before them' (9:1).

First of all, he recognizes that God is in sovereign control of the lives of his people. He holds them *in his hand* (9:1). We are reminded of the presentation of God's providence in Ecclesiastes 3, except that here the focus is deeply personalized. It defines the particular grace of God for all believers, one by one. They are known to him by name. His hands surround and guide their every breath. This concept of ever-present divine care is found

throughout Scripture. The holding of someone's hand speaks of *love* toward that person. Moses therefore confesses before God, 'Yes, he loves the people; all his saints are in your hand' (Deut. 33:3). The holding *up* of another's hand is an act

THINK ABOUT IT

THINK ABOUT IT

Is sin really real?

'Oh, I'm so sinful!' she says, as she stuffs the 'Death by Chocolate' dessert into her mouth. That is about as bad, or as real, as 'sin' gets in some people's thinking. 'Sin' is to be seen as a bad word, a creation of fuddy-duddy moralists. So modern usage of the word makes it no more dangerous than the playful indulgence of an occasional luxury.

1. Read Proverbs 14:9. Why does sin have to be made to look ridiculous, and a figment of overactive imaginations? How did the witches in Shakespeare's *Macbeth* handle 'foul' and 'fair' things — and why?

2. Read Romans 1:21-28 and work up a list* of what Paul says there about the nature and results of sin. Are these real or imaginary?

3. Read Romans 6:23 and ponder the fact that in God's 'dictionary' 'sin' is still a fatal pastime — and has only one remedy, whether for time or eternity.

*See Peter Jeffery, *Bitesize Theology* (Darlington: Evangelical Press, 2000), pp. 39-42.

of exaltation, as for example in the proclamation of a boxing champion. God's people are his *prize*, his jewels, even his regalia! 'You shall also be a crown of glory in the hand of the LORD, and a royal diadem in the hand of your God' (Isa. 62:3). Scripture also portrays God's hands as unbreakably holding his children and therefore surrounding them with an *everlasting security*. Jesus confirms this when he says of all believers, 'I give them eternal life, and they shall never perish; neither shall anyone snatch them out of my hand' (John 10:28).

Nevertheless, observes the writer, this does not guarantee an easy and comfortable life, because nobody knows whether love or hate waits for them in life's experiences (9:1). In other words, you cannot predict whether people will love you or hate you. God's love toward you does not guarantee that people will be fair to you and treat you well, far less love you. The world is full of free men and women who sin freely and do so in the face of their personal responsibility and God's revealed will and threatened judgements. God upholds believers in this potentially malicious milieu, but he does not promise them moonlight and roses! And no one needs persuading that the real experience of God's people is often very difficult indeed. Christians are not immune from the ordinary troubles that afflict the human race. We are strangers neither to heartache nor to personal failure.

Given these two facts of Christian life — the all-embracing providential care of God and the common human experience of the changing fortunes of life —

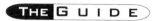

what then is the benefit of being a child of God? If our practical experience appears to have no obvious advantages, can it be said that there is any real evidence for our hope? Or is it all a meaningless exercise in self-deceit and wishful thinking?

'We're a' Jock Thamson's bairns!' (9:2-3)

WHAT THE TEXT TEACHES

When a Scot wants to emphasize that we human beings are all in the same boat in this fallen world, he says that we are all 'Jock Thamson's bairns'. Jock Thamson (John Thompson) is the common man and we are his 'bairns' (his little children). It is a way of saying to those who have pretensions to being something grand, that when all is said and done, as Robert Burns puts it, 'a man's a man for a' that'. The apostle Paul, quoting Greek poets to Athenian philosophers, explains it with magisterial simplicity, when he says we are all 'his offspring' (Acts 17:28-29). In practice this means that we all share a common destiny, whether good or bad, clean or unclean, churchgoers or not (9:2). The point is, as Michael Eaton observes, 'that the righteous are not visibly favoured by providence, nor the unrighteous visibly rebuked by providence'.[2]

The proof of this is that death — the ultimate providence — comes to all of us. This is the great evil under the sun (9:3). Death is not a normal part of life, like birth and childhood. It is an enemy and an evil. It is the wages of sin (Rom. 6:23). And it comes to all without discrimination or exception (Heb. 9:27).

But why has the Preacher led us from the idea of common humanity, to common experience, to death, and finally to sin? Why does sin have to come into the picture? Simply because it is impossible to analyse and understand the human condition and, specifically, the believer's experience in the world, apart from sin, condemnation and death.[3] The life of lost, unconverted sinners is characterized by 'evil' and 'madness' that signally affects both their lives and their destiny (9:3).

- Sin afflicts us from the *innermost depths* of our being — 'there is madness in their hearts'.
- It is a potentially *lifelong problem* — 'madness is in their hearts while they live'.
- This sin is not a part-time hobby but a matter of the most profound *devotion* — 'the hearts of the sons of men are full of evil'.

What this all adds up to is a terrifying, but sadly accurate view of the human condition, apart from spiritual rebirth and conversion to Christ through personal faith in him as Saviour. Charles Bridges, with shocking but holy honesty, says that 'it is impossible for the sinner to be more dangerously mad than he is, except by growing into greater wickedness'.[4] People dread mental illness with all its attendant problems. How much more should they flee from the madness of

unbelief in God and unrepentance toward the Lord Jesus Christ. The worst madness in the world is the mindset and heart commitment that runs from God to enlist with Satan's legion of spiritual terrorists. Sane sinners are in the grip of the most awesome insanity on earth, because it is a potentially endless madness that will be cooped up in a lost eternity, if there is no repentance toward God and faith in the Lord Jesus Christ.

While there's life, there's hope (9:4-6)

If the picture is as dismal as this, can hope be a practical possibility? If the Preacher is right — and who can refute him — how can anyone experience hope? The answer is implicit in the writer's method.

First, an illustration of the point at issue. Some years ago, a fit young athlete was admitted to Guy's Hospital in London, England, suffering from severe heart palpitations. So fast was the fibrillation that it was impossible to feel a pulse in the normal way. In fact, he broke the record for the highest heart rate in that hospital. The vital course of action was to get that pulse back down to normal before any permanent damage was done to the heart muscle. How did they do it? They applied massive electric shocks to the chest! And this did indeed do the trick. Our sinful condition is a heart problem as real but infinitely more serious than palpitations. And we need the shock treatment of God's Word to show us how dark are our hearts and how great is our danger! But with the shock comes the prospect of new life. Yes, there is hope! And it is to be found in how you respond to the Lord with the life he has given you, right now. The simple fact is that you only need to be alive to have hope! 'Anyone who is among the living has hope,' for, after all, 'even a live dog is better off than a dead lion!' (9:4, NIV). Death is the point of no return between time and eternity. You cannot live it over again if you wasted it the first time. And you cannot enjoy life in retrospect. Unlike pay increases, the enjoyment of life cannot be backdated! This is the Preacher's method — look at the realities of the human condition and face up to the fact that it is already happening to you — and then consider God's answer to the problem.

The finality of death casts its shadow over present activities and calls for some self-evaluation. 'The dead know nothing' (9:5). This is not to say there is no life after death, but only to emphasize the impossibility of undoing the past from across the great divide. Even the successes and rewards of wickedness in this life can only leave an eternally bitter aftertaste of what is lost for ever. The 'men of the world who have their portion in this life' (Ps. 17:14) is one of the great themes of Scripture. In the story of the rich man and Lazarus, Jesus has Abraham say to the rich man, who is in hell, 'Son, remember that in your lifetime you received your

good things' (Luke 16:25). What ought to have
been sought and received, modestly and moderately, as a blessing of God and a means of doing
others some good, became for the rich man his
summum bonum — his highest good and principal goal — and thus, in turn, became his god.
In death, the rich man knows his awful loss, but
in the Preacher's sense he 'know[s] nothing', for
he cannot cross the eternal chasm between this
world and eternity. There is 'no more reward,
for the memory of them is forgotten' (9:5).

The living, in contrast, have a great advantage. They 'know that they will die' (9:5)! The
sheer severity of the statement takes one's breath
away! We who are alive have hope because (the
Preacher argues) we know that we will die some
day! It seems almost trite or even derisive to suggest an idea like this. How can the inevitability
of death become an engine of living hope?

The answer is found in the nature of biblical
paradox. What seems so contradictory is in fact
inseparably related and, in the plan of God, is
designed to do us good. On an earlier occasion,
the Preacher told us that 'the day of death' is
better than 'the day of one's birth' (7:1). The
reason for this, as we saw, was in the paradox
that, if we are willing to think seriously about
these things, death reaches into our innermost
being in such a way as to profoundly change the
pattern of our future lives, whereas birthdays
represent backward-looking sentiment that has

no power to mould whatever future years God may give us. In other words, we can take the prospect of death, concentrate our minds on where we are now, and redeem the days ahead in devotion to the Lord. Then, as that sublime biblical expositor, Archbishop Robert Leighton, so beautifully expressed it, 'Death which cuts the sinews of all other hopes, and turns men out of all other inheritances, alone fulfills this hope, and ends it in fruition; as a messenger sent to bring the children of God home to the possession of their inheritance.'[5] So death, the enemy, is defeated by grace. And the first step in that transformation from defeat into victory is to look death squarely in the face *in God's terms* and realize that there is a life to live, in Jesus Christ, that death shall never conquer. This is true hope.

QUESTIONS FOR DISCUSSION

1. If we are in God's hands, why do we not know whether love or hate waits for us around the corner (9:1)? Do God's people have no security (see John 10:28)?

2. How ought we to respond to our common destiny (9:2-3)? Why are sane sinners in the grip of the most fearsome insanity on earth?

3. Discuss the story of the rich man and Lazarus (Luke 16:19-31) and show how it illustrates the point in 9:4-6, that while there is life, there is hope.

CHAPTER TWENTY

LIVING IN HOPE!

BIBLE READING

Ecclesiastes 9:7-10

As a practical rule of thumb most people probably think 'living in hope' is the capacity to put up with a daily life that is boring and unsatisfactory, while looking forward to the better days that will arrive in the future. Hope, to put it another way, is basically a survival technique that makes the frustrations of the present more bearable, even worthwhile. The greater the certainty of that hope becoming reality, the more acceptable the pain of waiting, as the Americans put it, 'for your ship to come in'.

This is undoubtedly and unavoidably an ingredient of all hope, since all deferred rewards cannot but be an incentive to persevere. Very little of any consequence is achieved in this life without some struggle. But no investment of pain and toil is sustained voluntarily for long without some hope of relief and return. And why should it be otherwise? Work, after all, is not an end in itself, but a means of providing for our needs and even our comfort. Who would plough and plant if there were no hope at all of a harvest? Surely not anyone with any sense in his head!

Solomon identifies four areas of living in which the spirit of hope produces a harvest of joy in the Lord — the joy that works the Lord's glory in us and increases our faith to overflowing: contentment (9:7), celebration (9:8), companionship (9:9), and commitment (9:10).

Contentment (9:7)

Contentment is God's mandate for our lives. The world, for the most part, derives its contentment *from* things, whereas Christians bring contentment *to* things. True contentment is an act of faith. It is a decision about our attitude based on obedience to God's stated will. It flows from personal godliness (1 Tim. 6:6). God never sanctions discontent, for discontent is the denial of faith, and without faith it is impossible to please God. The Preacher is emphatic. His word is a command from God: 'Go, eat your bread with joy...' (9:7). The gladness comes before the eating, not after it. 'Living hope' is the fruit, as Peter puts it, of the new birth 'through the resurrection of Jesus Christ from the dead' (1 Peter 1:3). It is the 'anchor of the soul, both sure and steadfast' (Heb. 6:19). It is therefore the organizing principle of the believer's attitude to life. That is why, in Christ, we shall be 'more than conquerors' (Rom. 8:37). When, in faith, we bring this heart attitude of contentment, which is living hope applied in advance to whatever comes upon our

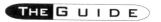

horizon, we will not be overwhelmed by the discouragements of the world, the flesh, or Satan himself. A Christian has no reason to complain![1]

And the reason for this is our acceptance by God: 'for God has already accepted your works' (9:7). Obedience is built upon acceptance, not acceptance upon obedience. We are called to righteous works, not to works-righteousness. We are not trying to persuade God to accept us; we are given the gift of living for him because we are already accepted, through faith in Christ.[2] We can expect blessing with open faces and joyous hearts.

Celebration (9:8)

Celebration must flow from the knowledge that God is pleased with what we do. Therefore, it is appropriate for God's people to clothe themselves with a spirit of cheerful praise. 'Let your garments always be white, and let your head lack no oil' (9:8). There is far more here than wearing clean clothes and looking after your complexion! In Scripture, white clothes are associated with the praise and the glory of God (see Mark 16:5; Matt. 17:2; Rev. 3:4,5,18; 19:8). They symbolize not purity — as most people assume, on account of white weddings — but victory. This was why the great Lutheran preacher, Philipp Jakob Spener (1635-1705), had himself buried in a white coffin! He was expressing his belief in the glorious future of the church of Jesus Christ.[3]

The practice of anointing the head with oil was a common feature of celebrations and feasts in the ancient world. This was the 'oil of joy' symbolic of the blessing of God (Ps. 45:8; Isa. 61:3). Christians ought to be the happiest people in the world. We have every reason to celebrate. Are we not saved by the Lord Jesus Christ? Do we not have a glorious destiny in Christ our Saviour? And if God be for us, who shall be against us?

Companionship (9:9)

Companionship in marriage is to be enjoyed. 'Live joyfully with the wife whom you love' (9:9; cf. 4:9-12). The shared life of husband and wife is designed by God to be a community of love and mutual support. The burdens of a meaningless life and meaningless days — i.e. life viewed as short and wracked with uncertainties — are not only shared but counteracted and turned to blessing. The rest of the verse, 'all the days of your vain life ... for that is your portion in life' (9:9) might sound dismal at first, but in fact the idea is thoroughly positive. This is 'your *portion* in life' tells us that a loving marriage partner is a wonderful gift of God. A portion in Scripture is a share in good things.[4] The writer stresses that we indeed live our lives out in what to others is no more than an 'under-the-sun' vain life, and contrasts the blessing of our 'portion' from the Lord with the emptiness around us.

Commitment (9:10)

After death, there is no way of doing what we ought to have done before. There is 'no work or

 THINK ABOUT IT

Getting the best out of night school

C. H. Spurgeon once wrote to a young lady, who was apparently discouraged over health problems, 'You seem to me to be in the night school — by no means pleasant lessons, few holidays, and no cakes and sugar-sticks — but a wise Teacher, and a guarantee of becoming a well-trained disciple in due time.'* Too many of us imagine that if we could only see more of the future, or have more light from the Lord on the present, then we would be more lively, faithful and hopeful Christians. No, says Spurgeon, 'Too much sight renders faith impossible. A certain measure of darkness is needful for the full exercise of faith. Be of good comfort; for He who has redeemed you will not lose that which has cost Him so much.'

Read Romans 8:18-30, and then reflect carefully on verses 24-25. When does hope function most powerfully in our experience? When will we 'wait for it [salvation] with perseverance'? Answer: when 'we hope for what we do not see'. Less sight + faith in Christ = more hope. Compare Hebrews 11:1.

* Iain H. Murray (ed), *Letters of Charles Haddon Spurgeon* (Edinburgh: Banner of Truth, 1992), p. 75.

device or knowledge or wisdom in the grave where you are going' (9:10). Therefore, redeeming the time and claiming the fruits of the life God has given us requires energetic application (working), practical strategies (planning), informed accomplishment (knowledge), and skilful execution (wisdom). 'Whatever your hand finds to do, do it with your might' (9:10). There is no room here for a flee-the-world mentality. Because this is God's world, God's people have the mandate of heaven to live joyfully, hopefully and fruitfully as they claim through their work and witness the dominion over the creation that God gave man from the beginning (Gen. 1:28). God's children have work to do and a world to win. And the motivating power for our commitment to life comes from the Saviour, who is 'Christ in [us], the hope of glory' (Col. 1:27). Christians know where they are going, and they know who is going with them. John Owen, one of the greatest English theologians, points out that 'hope in general' is no more than 'an uncertain expectation of a future good which we desire'. In contrast, the Christian hope, in Jesus Christ, is 'a gospel grace' and therefore 'an earnest expectation, proceeding from faith, trust and confidence, accompanied by longing desires of enjoyment'.[5] For this reason, the uncertainty is removed and a vision of the fruitfulness of discipleship to Christ takes centre stage in the mind and motivation of the believer. We live in hope, because Christ, who is the hope of glory, lives in us by the Holy Spirit.

Hoping in Christ

First of all, Christian hope *anticipates the believer's future reward*. This, in the nature of the case, is its basic underlying character. Moses regarded 'the reproach of Christ greater riches than the treasures of Egypt'. Why? Because 'he looked to the reward' (Heb. 11:26). Indeed, all the faithful folk mentioned in Hebrews 11 are commended for their faith precisely because they persevered toward the goal of the promised reward. Even so, not one of them actually received what had been promised (Heb. 11:39), because these promises pertained to Christ and an era way into the future. They were, however, not without real blessings in their lives. There are many promises of God besides those which prophesied to the Old Testament believers about the coming of the Lord Jesus Christ and which promises heaven to us New Testament Christians. But they are all in the nature of rewards, and the incentive of reward, however centred in spiritual things, is not to be despised as an unworthy motivation in the Christian's heart.

Such motivation need be no more carnal and self-seeking than the grace that provides the reward of redemption in Christ. It is certainly possible to seek God's blessings with utterly self-centred motives. This is part of the story of human sin, and the Bible is filled with examples of people who tried to gain favour with God through self-centred and self-righteous means — from Cain to Saul and from the Pharisees to Ananias and Sapphira. But to have a holy vision of the glory that God will yet reveal for us and in us, through our Saviour, the Lord Jesus Christ, is simply the bedrock of all true Christian hope. With Moses, we rightly look ahead to our reward, and with Paul, we joyously anticipate an eternal glory that will outweigh any present troubles (2 Cor. 4:17).

Secondly, Christian hope *enlivens the believer's present experience.* Hope in Jesus Christ is not 'pie in the sky, by and by', but embraces another dimension of reward that deepens and enriches the daily living of life far in advance of heaven and the eternal reward of unfading glory. Perhaps this distinction is best illustrated from the life of Jesus. John's Gospel records Jesus' 'great high priestly prayer' on the last night he spent with the disciples prior to his death on the cross. In that prayer he says to his Father, 'And the glory which you gave me I have given them [the disciples]' (John 17:22). Then, in almost the next breath, he prays, 'Father, I desire that they also whom you gave me may be with me where I am, that they may behold my glory which you have given me; for you loved me before the foundation of the world' (John 17:24).

Clearly these are two different manifestations of the same glory. The first has already been given to the church on earth; the second awaits them in heaven with Jesus. The latter is the eternal state of glory in the presence of God, while the former refers to the spiritual experience of believers in this life. But what does Jesus have in mind here? What glory did he have that he gave to his disciples? Surely it was the glory of his holiness and righteousness as the suffering servant of the Lord! And this is the glory of the church after Pentecost — the glory of sharing in Christ's triumph over sin, through a life of commitment to him in lively faith. It is the glory of the paradox that the world sees but cannot quite fathom, namely, that being Christ-like means sharing the fellowship of his sufferings and thereby sharing in his redeeming victory (1 Peter 4:13).

The fulness of the Christian gospel was not in the Preacher's mind as he wrote the Book of Ecclesiastes. Yet, apart from the explicit Christ-centredness of New Testament teaching on the Christian life and hope, his picture of the way we ought to live breathes precisely the same spirit in which godly hope is to be lived out today by Christians. He addresses the question of how we can live in hope, namely, how hope can raise us above the disappointments and frustrations of life in responding to *real situations*, as opposed to merely enduring them until we come to heaven. To live in hope is to experience the glory that Jesus gives *now*, while we also wait expectantly for the glory he will give later in heaven when we shall see him as he is (1 John 3:2).

QUESTIONS FOR DISCUSSION

1. How are we to 'live in hope'? Identify the four areas of living in which hope produces a harvest of joy in the Lord and discuss their importance in daily living.

2. Is the expectation of reward an unworthy motive in the Christian life? Discuss 1 Timothy 6:6. List your expectations from a life of following Jesus.

3. What is the only sure basis for hope? What kinds of 'hope' do millions of people entertain? Are they real or are they illusions?

CHAPTER
TWENTY-ONE

YOU ARE ONLY
HUMAN!

LOOK IT
UP

BIBLE READING

Ecclesiastes 9:11-18

INTRODUCTION

When a triumphant Roman general returned from a successful campaign, he might, if notably successful, be accorded a 'triumph'. This was the pinnacle of state and public recognition for a soldier. He and his troops, together with their captives and the spoils of war, marched in procession through the streets of Rome to receive the plaudits of the populace. During the procession the general was accompanied by a slave, who stood at his shoulder and, lest the hero should be tempted to think himself a god, repeated in his ear the words, 'Remember you are human!'

We all need to be reminded of our limitations. It was foolish of Eve to entertain the lie of the serpent, when he assured her that a bite of the forbidden fruit would open her eyes so that she would be 'like God, knowing good and evil' (Gen. 3:5). Moderns are too subtle and rationalistic to lay any claims to divinity, but the truth is that to reject the living God is to enthrone man as if he were God — the ultimate adjudicator of what is good and what is bad. In such circumstances, man is his own god, and because he views himself as the ultimate authority, he has already forgotten the true parameters of human limitation. Instead of wisdom, he generates schemes; for moral absolutes he substitutes relativism and the majority vote; and in place of God's revealed truth, the shifting sand of under-the-sun opinion. There is only one alternative to the worship of God, and that is the idolatry of man, whether expressed through man-made religions or man-made secular philosophies. And such idolatry is the most profound foolishness in the universe (Ps. 14:1; Rom. 1:21-23). Insofar as man rejects God both for who he is and for what he reveals for our blessing, man also rejects his true humanness and pretends to an ultimacy completely beyond his essential creaturehood.

Ecclesiastes lays out for us the consequences of forgetting what it means to be truly human. A thread of delicious irony is woven very deftly through the presentation of this theme. It is the notion that when man sees his humanness exclusively as an under-the-sun (secular, godless) humanism, he actually loses the essential perspective that defines both *who* he is and *what* constitutes his true calling and destiny. Denying the wisdom of God and his relationship to him as the creature to his Creator, he embraces the very opposite (under-the-sun meaninglessness) as the conventional wisdom for the new humanity, independent of God and alone in the universe.

WHAT THE TEXT TEACHES

The Preacher is therefore at pains to remind us of our human frailty and our need to depend upon the Lord. He enters some cautions about the limits of wisdom. He has just been speaking of what it means to live in hope. He talked of contentment, celebration, companionship and commitment (9:7-10). It was a vision for the enjoyment of life as the gift of God. And it was neither fantasy nor wishful thinking but a mandate from God based upon the personal acceptance of each believer by God. God 'has already accepted your works' (9:7). A distinction has to be drawn, however, between God's mandate for our lives and God's providence in our lives. We are given gifts to use, things to do, and promises to claim, all to be lived out in faith, hope and love, with the joy of the Lord in our hearts. We can expect blessing! But the world into which we go is not always friendly and the life of faith even runs smack into 'the gates of hell' (Matt. 16:18). Jesus says it clearly, 'In the world you will have tribulation' (John 16:33). He also says, in the same breath, not to be afraid because he has 'overcome the world'. As far as our experience of life is concerned, the overcoming is after, not before, the trouble. We must not isolate one aspect of God's promises and ignore the others. We must remember that victory only comes with a battle and somebody else's defeat! The favour of God is not a panacea for the ills of the times.

Christians will go on living lives of vibrant faith, victorious hope and exultant joy in their Saviour, but they will still have plenty of obstacles in their way. The key to keeping your balance is never to be caught on the wrong foot. Spiritual balance comes from having two feet firmly planted on the Rock that is Jesus Christ (1 Cor. 10:4; Matt. 16:18): 'On Christ the solid rock I stand, All other ground is sinking sand' (Edward Mote).

The Preacher then gives four points about wisdom to illustrate our need for balanced and realistic expectations in life.

Accomplishments do not guarantee success (9:11)

Five quick-fire examples spring from the Preacher's pen:

> The race is not to the swift,
> Nor the battle to the strong,
> Nor bread to the wise
> Nor riches to men of understanding,
> Nor favour to men of skill (9:11).

The reason is that 'time and chance happen to them all' (9:11). This is just to say that things are taking place out of our sight and beyond our foresight that dramatically reverse our natural expectations. God knows but we do not. Even our wisest preparations can be little

THINK ABOUT IT

'Have you ever met an uneducated atheist?'

The British scientist, Richard Dawkins, penned these breathtaking words in a 1996 newspaper article. He also described belief in God as 'ignominious, contemptible and retarded'. Commenting on this, John Blanchard counters with an equally breathtaking comment. 'There is a tragic irony here. Far from being able to make dogmatic assertions about the most important issues in life, *fallen man is fundamentally incapable of valid insight about anything.'** Quoting Psalm 10:4,6,13, he points out that atheism and pride 'have always been a perfect fit for each other'. Look up the following Scriptures and note the connections.

1. Proverbs 27:1: Don't … because you don't…

2. Romans 1:18: The … is suppressed in …

3. Romans 1:22: They say they are … , but are…

4. Romans 1:24: They exchanged the … of God for the…

5. Romans 1:28: They rejected … and their minds became…

What does God say here about the 'knowledge' and 'wisdom' that leaves him out of the picture? Carefully work through Romans 11:33-34 and Ephesians 3:8-12, noting what is said about the connection of true wisdom and knowing Christ as your own Saviour.

Memorize Psalm 119:97-100

* J. Blanchard, *Does God believe in atheists?* (Darlington: Evangelical Press, 2000), p. 495.

better than jumping to false conclusions. Whatever our gift, whether speed, strength, or wisdom, it is a fallacy to put our trust in it and forget meanwhile that other factors are involved — not least the sovereign purposes of God. He sees to it that 'pride goes before destruction, and a haughty spirit before a fall' (Prov. 16:18).

The prophet Habakkuk complained to the Lord that he had let a 'wicked foe' succeed in his oppression of the righteous. This successful exploiter of the weak was like a fisherman. He cast his net, gathered up his harvest, and was understandably elated because he could live a life of luxury and enjoy the best that this world could offer. And to what or whom was he thankful for this vile success? 'Therefore they sacrifice to their net, and burn incense to their dragnet; because by them their share is sumptuous and their food plentiful' (Hab. 1:16). He trusts in his net, and in his own abilities. And he uses them to serve his own selfish and unscrupulous purposes.

What Habakkuk is condemning in the wicked, the Preacher is gently urging believers to avoid. Don't trust in your net! Don't think that even the personal gifts that God has given you guarantee trouble-free progress in life. Don't trust the gift. Trust in the Giver! Then you will see the Lord do great things through you.

Ignorance of the future (9:12)

'An evil time' can 'fall suddenly' upon us (9:12). We are incapable of controlling the flow of our own lives,

however much we plan and however great our talents may be. All of us expect in practice to get up tomorrow morning and get on with a new day. Individuals and great nations live as if they will go on indefinitely. For example, who would have believed at that time, that in a short space of years, a few thousand Greeks and their youthful king, Alexander, would sweep the mighty Persian empire away for ever? Who really believed the collapse of Communism would occur as it did in 1993? Our abilities and our wisdom cannot secure our future from unexpected turns. Our only security is the Lord and his promise never to allow us to be separated from his love. Paul recognized the reality of both sides of the equation — uncertainty about future events and certainty, in the Lord, about future destiny — when he declared his conviction that 'neither death nor life, nor angels nor principalities nor powers, nor things present nor things to come, nor height nor depth, nor any other created thing, shall be able to separate us from the love of God which is in Christ Jesus our Lord' (Rom. 8:38-39). We may be human, but there is a God in heaven!

Wisdom is frequently unrecognized (9:13-16)

Consider the case of a 'poor wise man' who saved a city when it had been besieged by a powerful enemy. We are not told how he did it, but 'he by his wisdom delivered the city' and was then promptly forgotten (9:15). What conclusions ought we to draw from this? First, that wisdom is to be prized as a great gift; but, second, that you had better be prepared for some disappointments. If you expect that being wise, stating the truth, and explaining the obvious will gain you the attention, approval and influence you feel you should receive, then you just have not reckoned with the way of the real world. You have forgotten that you are living in a fallen world where sin has blinded many hearts and foolishness is legal tender in the marketplace of ideas.

Wisdom is very often overthrown (9:17-18)

People will listen to 'the shout of a ruler of fools' — the Israelite version of a rabble-rousing local politician — when they should listen to 'words of the wise, spoken quietly' (9:17). Noise attracts attention, whether from politicians or preachers. Quietness is unexciting and, for many people, gentle thoughtfulness is associated with wimpishness. In Scripture, quietness is the constant characteristic of the relationship between the Lord and his believing people. 'Be still, and know that I am God,' says the psalmist (Ps. 46:10). Jesus' ministry was quietly delivered and heard in quietness by his disciples. Jesus did not 'quarrel nor cry out; nor will anyone hear his voice in the streets' (Matt. 12:19). The Lord

is not always quiet, it is true. But when he thunders, it is to dispense his judgements and declare his glory.[1]

The message for us is that true wisdom is at a premium — it is better than aircraft carriers and nuclear missiles (9:18). The truth of this claim, comments Ernest Hengstenberg, 'would show itself in the example of the powers of the world if they only lent an ear to its voice, and it will one day be proved in the experience of the nation whose privilege it is to possess wisdom, in the day when, notwithstanding its defenceless impotence it is raised to universal dominion'.[2] That nation is, of course, the 'holy nation' — the church of the Lord Christ (1 Peter 2:9).

A sinister caveat concludes the discussion of the limitations of wisdom and forms a bridge to the succeeding discussion of folly. However precious wisdom may be, it only takes 'one sinner' to destroy 'much good' (9:18). In a fallen world wisdom is always swimming upstream. Sin runs with the current. Sin has all the natural advantages. It does not need conversions and changed hearts. Wisdom, on the other hand, needs the actual intervention of the Holy Spirit! This is not to minimize the power of the gospel to change men and women. It is simply to explain why we see sin so rampant in the world (see 1 Kings 22:52; 1 Cor. 5:6; 15:33; Heb. 12:15).

Is the Preacher perhaps too doleful and even destructive in the way he assesses our limitations? Someone might be forgiven for thinking this of him, at least on a first reading. Yet surely no one can say that his observations of the way the world actually is, the way we actually behave, and what the Lord's people actually experience in the world are inaccurate. He speaks for God. He gives the heaven's-eye view of life on earth. And his purpose is that we might live for God. Behind it all lies a vision of the limitless power of God's grace, which reaches into our lives to transform and sustain us. But we must reckon honestly with our human limitations, if his strength is to be made perfect in our weakness (2 Cor. 12:9).

QUESTIONS FOR DISCUSSION

1. Why do we need to be reminded of our limitations?

2. Discuss the four limits of wisdom in 9:11-18:

   a. Why are gifts and success so often a snare (v. 11)?
   b. Do we really know the future (v. 12)?
   c. Is wisdom always recognized as wise (vv. 13-16)?
   d. What can happen to wisdom in this world (vv. 17-18)?

3. How does this apply to the secular-humanist faith that (secular) education will solve the world's problems?

CHAPTER
TWENTY-TWO

THE HEART OF
FOLLY

BIBLE READING

Ecclesiastes 10

It is said that Admiral Sir John Jellicoe was the only man who could have lost World War I in an afternoon.[1] The reason for this was that he commanded Britain's Grand Fleet — the steel wall of battleships that secured command of the world's oceans. Defeat for the Royal Navy would simply have meant the end of the Allied war effort. So every time Jellicoe took his fleet to sea, he knew that it would take just one foolish mistake to deliver the Allied cause into the hands of the Kaiser's Germany. The day of testing finally dawned on 31 May 1916, off Jutland, Denmark. When it was done, Britannia still ruled the waves, even though she lost more ships and men than the Germans. Admiral Jellicoe had been prepared. He did not lose the war that day, or any other day.

The contours of folly (10:1-3)

A sober mind is needed in a crisis if mistakes are not to be made. Foolish actions can do a great deal of damage. The Preacher therefore takes us to the heart of the matter to provide us with a brief but penetrating review of three of the most basic practical characteristics of human folly.

1. Folly's small beginning (10:1)

A little folly goes a long way. It is like flies in the ointment — just 'a little' outweighs 'wisdom and honour' (10:1). Perhaps we can still remember the shame we felt at some time in the past when we said or did something, possibly in jest or even with good intentions, only to cause hurt to our friends and cast a shadow over our personal integrity. Personal friendships have dissolved into bitterness over a single silly remark. Many lives have been devastated because of that extra couple of drinks on the way home from the office. All it takes is one fly in the ointment.

Knowing the potential dangers ought to set us thinking about damage control strategies in advance. This is most immediately applicable to our individual personality traits and known foibles. Quick tempers and quicksilver tongues need training and self-control to head off rash outbursts. The apostle Paul speaks of beating his body and making it his slave — a figurative way of describing the cultivation of personal holiness with its constant need of dying to sin and living in the Holy Spirit (1 Cor. 9:27; Rom. 8:13). We need to forearm ourselves against the plunderings of our own frailties.

Once that self-discipline is in place, there is still no scope for relaxed vigilance. We must be prepared at all

times (2 Tim. 4:2); we must watch and pray in case we fall into temptation (Mark 14:38); and we must, like Gideon's soldiers at the brook, be ready for action even as we refresh ourselves (Judges 7:5-7). So the Preacher is urging believers to prepare for victory rather than court defeat. Keep a clear focus on your calling and duty and be vigilant to squash the first appearance of foolishness.

2. Folly is a matter of the heart (10:2)

'A wise man's heart is at his right hand, but a fool's heart at his left' (10:2). In Hebrew, the word 'heart' denotes the innermost nature of a person — what we are, what we really think, what drives us and motivates us. The unmentioned watershed between the two is what the old writers, like the Anglican evangelical Charles Bridges, call 'the keeping of the heart with God'.[2] In Scripture, the right hand side is connected with blessing and honour (Ps. 16:8; Matt. 25:34, 41). The divergent paths of right and left, therefore, are a figurative way of saying that the wise and the foolish start from different precommitments and will inevitably chart separate courses to radically opposing goals. The Preacher wishes to impress upon his readers that foolishness should not be shrugged off as tolerable and harmless. It is not 'just one of those things' to be accepted as a normal (and acceptable within limits) part of life.

Rather, we ought to be sensitive to the depth of the problem and its far-reaching long-term consequences. The reason there is 'no fool like an old fool' is that the young fools never changed their ways!

3. Folly will out (10:3)

Eventually folly is seen for what it is. This is the nearest the Preacher comes to humour in the whole book: 'Even when a fool walks along the way, he lacks wisdom, and he shows everyone that he is a fool' (10:3). He is an unfunny comedian. A professional comic is funny because he is a clever caricature of the fool. But the fool is ultimately a tragedy because he cannot see himself as he really is. When he thinks his actions are sound and reasonable, they are in fact evidently deficient. The picture of the fool as a man who cannot even walk along the road without betraying himself is apt. He is like the emperor who had no clothes, but blithely paraded before his subjects in the belief that he was dressed in the most magnificent finery!

Insights on folly (10:4-20)

The remainder of the chapter is a pot-pourri of proverbial observations about foolishness and its consequences. All are from daily life, and we are bound to run into them sooner or later. The Preacher clearly intends that we should spot what not to do, and, although he does not come out and say it until the last

THINK ABOUT IT

Answering fools in their folly

Proverbs 26:4-5: *Do not answer a fool according to his folly, lest you also be like him. Answer a fool according to his folly, lest he be wise in his own eyes.*

G. K. Chesterton once said that a paradox is 'truth stood on its head to get our attention'. Proverbs 26:4-5 surely gets our attention. But is there maybe a fatal contradiction here? Clearly Solomon does not think so, for he offers them as equally valid statements. What is the answer? Just that if you are going to challenge a fool, you should consider two vitally important things: mode and motive.

1. *The mode*: care about your own spiritual state (v. 4). Be careful not to follow the fool's agenda, or to trade punches with him on his terms. If you do, you will have compromised yourself and your message. The Christian that takes up worldliness to advance godliness is obviously being foolish. The world sees that in a moment and uses it to brush off what you have to say. Stupidity in God's people gives occasion for the enemies of the Lord to blaspheme (2 Sam. 12:14; cf. 1 Tim. 5:14). You won't save a drowning man by drowning yourself. You must hold the high ground with transparent integrity and grace. If you can't do that, you might as well shut up. You're the one that needs the help.

2. *The motive*: care about the fool's spiritual state! (v. 5). Your interest is not to be in scoring points for yourself and puffing yourself up with self-importance. It is to save a man from the consequences of will-worship and self-deceit. It is axiomatic that the fool thinks he is wise. That is what Paul highlights in 1 Cor. 1:18ff — and the thrust is that 'the foolishness of God is wiser than men'. The tragedy of the fool is that he is blind to his foolishness and therefore is in for a big shock if his eyes are not opened and his heart changed. The gospel of Christ is the 'wisdom' of God that is 'foolishness' with men. Christ *is* the power of God and the wisdom of God, who is made for all who will trust in him, 'wisdom from God — and righteousness and sanctification and redemption' (1 Cor. 1:24,30).

chapter of his book, he is challenging us to trust in God for wisdom in the face of life's trials. Many practical points are made, in no particular order, and these touch us as personally as they must have touched the people of Israel two millennia ago.

1. Evil arises from fools in government (10:4-7)

Only twice in this entire chapter do the Preacher's rather wistful musings rise to the imperatives of command. Both occasions involve being very careful indeed in the way we deal with the authorities (see 10:4; 10:20). This first case pictures a civil servant who is subjected to the (presumably unjustified) anger of a ruler. He is urged to respond calmly and stay at his post, for 'conciliation pacifies great offences' (10:4). The obverse has been noted by the English poet, George Herbert:

> Be calm in arguing; for fierceness makes
> Error a fault, and truth discourtesy.[3]

The Preacher is not saying we should all be doormats and let everything go by without a word. But grace and practical wisdom can be allies. After all, it can be dangerous to face up to an angry and powerful superior, even if you are in the right! Why stoke the fire when it is already overheating?

Still worse is a situation where folly and incompetence become entrenched and even rewarded in the corridors of power (10:5-7). In such aggravated

WHAT THE TEXT TEACHES

circumstances, where the 'servants' ride 'on horses' and 'princes walk on the ground like servants' (10:7), calmness and loyalty would be severely tested. Bad government breeds discontent and disloyalty and is 'an evil' (10:5). The Preacher offers no further analysis, far less advice, and his silence seems ominous. When we are ruled by fools, we need to know that there is a God who is truly sovereign over his creation and that 'the king's heart is in the hand of the LORD, like the rivers of water; he turns it wherever he wishes' (Prov. 21:1). Remembering our humanity is only meaningful when we remember there is a God.

2. Vindictiveness returns like a boomerang (10:8)

Dig a pit for somebody and you may fall in yourself! Many a terrorist has been blown up by the bomb he meant for his victims. Just as God promises that his blessing will follow acts of genuine kindness, so he warns of the destructive consequences of maliciousness (Ps. 7:14-16; Prov. 11:3-6; 12:3; 28:10). Our Lord enunciated the basic principle when, at the time of his arrest in the Garden of Gethsemane, he rebuked Peter for striking one of the high priest's men with his sword: 'all who take the sword will perish by the sword' (Matt. 26:52). It was this just principle that was applied in the case of Haman, who attempted an Old Testament holocaust by plotting the extinction of the Jews in the Persian Empire. He failed and was hanged on the gallows he had built for the Jewish leader, Mordecai (Esther 7:10). Similarly, the men who had Daniel thrown into the lions' den were later to die in the jaws of the very same animals (Dan. 24). Sin, like a rubber ball, will come bouncing back to you before too long! When we remember who we are, as people called to serve God, we will seek first the kingdom of God and his righteousness and repent of the sin that — outside of the grace of Jesus Christ, which cleanses, forgives and renews — would bring us down to self-destruction.

3. Thoughtfulness pays dividends (10:9-10)

In my Scottish youth, we lived three floors above the shop of Jimmy Knott the fishmonger. He was a real 'blether' — he talked endlessly and entertainingly with all and sundry, including us boys. What amazed us was that, as he talked on and on, he filleted his fish at lightning speed and never seemed to look at what he was doing! Yet that razor sharp knife never seemed to as much as nick a finger! Off came the head ... the tail ... the guts ... the skin ... and presto, a beautifully symmetrical fillet! Jimmy Knott's dextrous fingers were a living parable of the value of lots of good practice. 'Skill will bring success' (10:10, NIV). The Preacher applies this to the mind. Just as the unsharpened axe — or fishmonger's knife — can only make the job more difficult, if not even hazardous, so the unthinking mind will hinder a person's progress and usefulness. 'Look

before you leap,' says the proverb. It is foolishness not to think things through, but 'wisdom' — the greatest of all skills — 'brings success'.

4. Don't slacken off! (10:11)

A snake charmer can be a skilful practitioner of his trade, but if he loses concentration and fails to establish control over the snake, the consequences can be very nasty indeed. Slackness can be the death of skill. Ability is a bit like a steak on the grill — neglect it long enough and it will all go up in smoke. It is not enough to have talent. It is easily lost. A wise man will keep his wits about him. Remembering our humanity, under God, awakens us to a lively and vigilant spirit. 'Therefore let us not sleep, as others do, but let us watch and be sober...' says Paul. 'For God did not appoint us to wrath, but to obtain salvation through our Lord Jesus Christ' (1 Thess. 5:6,9).

5. No! They aren't 'just words'! (10:12-14)

The things we say can often reveal very effectively the kind of people we are: 'The words of a wise man's mouth are gracious, but the lips of a fool shall swallow him up' (10:12). The contrast is apposite, for it shows that the essential difference between the two is that, whereas the words of the wise *go out* and communicate grace to

others, the words of the fool turn *inward* and produce
a harvest of *self-destruction*. It is important to remember that, in Scripture, a fool is not someone who is dull
and unintelligent, but someone who is 'wrong-headed'
in that 'his thinking (and therefore his speaking) refuses
to begin with God'.[4] From his presuppositions to his
philosophy and theology, to his attitudes, actions and
words, everything is pointing in the wrong direction
— away from the path of blessing as revealed by God.
And the longer he goes on in this way, the deeper he
gets into the mire. To begin with, these words are 'foolishness' (10:13) — perhaps something ill-advised or
silly, but not too important when considered in isolation. Who, after all, goes through life without saying
something foolish? But this is a way of life for the fool.
It ends as 'wicked madness' — 'an irrationality which
is morally perverse'.[5] He 'multiplies words' (10:14), but
has no real basis for any confidence he has in them. He
has no knowledge of what the future holds. But when
did that ever stop a fool from building castles in the air
(10:14; cf. James 4:13; Luke 12:18-20)? Think, then,
about what you are saying — it is not 'just words'.
Remember that 'the heart of the righteous studies how
to answer, but the mouth of the wicked pours forth evil'
(Prov. 15:28).

6. A fool's work wearies him (10:15)

When it comes to actions, and particularly the consist-
ency and competency required to do productive work,
the fool is also found wanting. As with his words, so

also with his deeds. He has no inner guidance system. He therefore does not know 'how to go to the city' (10:15): plan, goals, and things. Indeed, what George Grant has called 'his moral catatonia' — i.e. 'wasteful and irresponsible behaviour' — will eventually 'drive him over the edge of responsibility, prosperity, and sanity'.[6] This is a word to the wise.

7. Exercise practical political wisdom (10:16-20)

The Preacher returns once more to the problem of irresponsible and incompetent rulers, the theme first taken up in verses 4-7. The bones are virtually identical, although the flesh is somewhat fuller of form. What earlier was described as 'an evil' is now intensified to a prophetic declaration of an imminent curse: '*Woe* to you, O land, when your king is a child...' (10:16; see Isa. 3:1-5). The contrast between this and the blessing of a land whose king 'is the son of nobles' serves to emphasize the former nation's predicament even more darkly (10:17). The indicator of the fitness or otherwise of the two monarchs respectively is the way they eat! The prince who feasts in the morning shows his lack of interest in governing his realm; his stickability is missing. He may be talkative enough and have endless energy to embark on new schemes, but for all that he is gripped by what Michael Eaton trenchantly defines as 'a moral and intellectual laziness which leads to a stumbling (2:14), fumbling (10:2), crumbling (10:18) life.'[7] He is a biblical sluggard. If he is energetic, it is not for the right he obviously wants to live a luxurious life, unhindered by any necessity to work and exercise responsibility. On the other hand, the good king eats 'at the proper time' — for strength and not debauchery.

The incompetence of the foolish is not rewarded with a lightning bolt of divine judgement, but with the steady decay of life's infrastructure. Just as the fool is consumed by his own words (10:12), so his irresponsible actions cannibalize the very fabric of his existence. He consumes without producing! 'Because of laziness the building decays, and through idleness of hands the house leaks' (10:18).

That is also the way with governments and nations, as much as it is for individuals. The self-serving attitude appears to be summed up in 10:19 — the debauched rulers declare their manifesto even as they feast on the legalized pillage extracted from their misgoverned and oppressed subjects: 'A feast is made for laughter, and wine makes merry; but money answers everything.' Food, wine and money are all there is for such people. This is the meaning of life! This is the goal of the voluptuary, the *summum bonum* of the under-the-sun 'good life'. Eat, drink, and be merry ... for there is no real tomorrow!

The Preacher assumes that this will be an ongoing fact of life. His parting counsel is to chart a calm and careful course in relation to the authorities and the big money interests. Don't let them get to you so that you

start being foolish and therefore bring unneces-
sary troubles upon yourself. Keep your own
counsel. Be circumspect in your thoughts. Don't
even curse the rich in the privacy of your bed-
room, because 'a bird of the air may carry your
voice' (10:20). It should be clear from the general thrust of Ecclesiastes that the writer cannot
be advising us to abandon all principles just so
that we can survive. The context is a discussion
of foolishness, and he is simply advocating not
doing anything foolish. Martyrdom may come
soon enough. And if it comes, let it be for good,
God-honouring reasons. The criticism of even a
tyrant is not an example of the kind of righteousness for which Christians might be persecuted.
Picking a fight is not the same as standing for
the truth. He therefore urges a quiet wisdom that
thinks before it acts and trusts the Lord at every
point along the way.

A young lad was going off for a summer job
on board a ship plying the Great Lakes. His father
had been a merchant seaman before he had
become a minister of the gospel, and he was con-
scious of the dangers and temptations of life on
the ocean wave. So he gave him a few words of
advice. They were few, maybe, but very well
chosen: 'Son, keep your eyes open, keep your
nose clean, keep your mouth shut, keep your
head down, and read the Book of Proverbs again
and again!' That is, in essence, what God is saying to us through his servant the Preacher.

QUESTIONS FOR DISCUSSION

1. *Identify the three basic characteristics of human folly in 10:1-3.*

2. *Review the seven practical points made about folly and wisdom in 10:4-22.*
   a. *Is 'government' always good (10:4-7)?*
   b. *What about taking the law into your own hands (10:8)?*
   c. *Is practice not just drudgery (10:9-10)?*
   d. *Can we never slacken off a little bit (10:11)?*
   e. *Is anything 'just words' (10:12-14)?*
   f. *Can we be too serious about work (10:15)?*
   g. *Discuss practical political wisdom in action (10:16-22).*

3. *Discuss 'Answering fools in their folly' (Prov. 26:4-5).*

THE GUIDE

CHAPTER
TWENTY-THREE

LIVE BY FAITH!

LOOK IT UP

BIBLE READING

Ecclesiastes 11:1-6

INTRODUCTION

One of the advantages of an invitation to be a guest preacher on one of the small islands off the west coast of Scotland is that the sail on the ferry offers a time of leisurely contemplation in beautiful scenery with lots of wonderfully fresh sea air. On one such occasion — it was a lovely autumn day — I noticed that a number of passengers on the promenade deck were throwing pieces of their sandwiches into the water. The text, 'Cast your bread upon the waters,' instantly came to my mind. It was obvious, however, that this bread was not going to come back 'after many days'. Much of it was scooped up by the sea gulls even before it hit the sea! Even so, it struck me that in a sense the bread did return to those who threw it over the side. The return was to see the skill, the sheer poetry of motion of the gulls as they wheeled and swooped around the ship. We enjoyed their enjoyment! We enjoyed the beauty of God's creatures.

There is probably a more literal basis than this for the Preacher's expression. The time for sowing seed in the Nile delta in the years before controlled irrigation was to wait until the annual inundation and then, as the waters went down, to cast the seed onto the water. It would disappear into the soil then being deposited. But, in due course, it germinated and produced a rich harvest. The 'bread' in the form of seed[1] must be hidden in the soil in the expectation of the later return of next year's 'daily bread'.

The central idea is that of faith-commitment of one's resources toward a future of productivity and blessing. Commerce and business also provide a model that illustrates this point. It takes 'bread' (in the modern idiom, a reference to money or capital) to make an investment in a new business. And it takes a degree of trust to venture that capital into the uncertain seas of the commercial world.

The Preacher is concerned with the meaning and direction of life. He began by considering the secular, under-the-sun life — life lived without any regard to God and eternity — and found it to be meaningless. In this, he echoed the despair expressed by those who saw no way out of the tragedies and anomalies of their existence. He agreed with those who found the under-the-sun life inherently meaningless. He agreed that death is a wall the secularist concept of meaning cannot climb. Through ten chapters, he exhumes the corpse of humanism (this-world-only, no-future-beyond-the-grave, godless secularism in all its forms) and with relentless logic, shows us that it is really dead. He has demonstrated that the industrious inventiveness of self-proclaimed autonomous man to carve meaning for

himself from life on planet Earth is little more than the twitchings and spasms of spiritual death. Interwoven throughout his exposition of meaninglessness is an emergent tapestry of rising hope that points to God's alternatives to man's prevailing predicament. The last two chapters of Ecclesiastes call for decisions to be God's disciples and to live in faith for him. The writer's tone changes from the sombre to the triumphant, from a darkling pessimism to a luminous hope, rising to a ringing crescendo: 'Fear God and keep his commandments, for this is the whole duty of man' (12:13, NIV).

Ecclesiastes 11 challenges us to invest in life with a vigorous holy boldness and with a joyous and expectant spirit. Living for the Lord *is* the good life. It is the happy life, for it rests securely upon the salvation God has wrought for all who will love him.

Life is a faith venture (11:1)

Casting your bread upon the waters is not an option, but a divine imperative. It is also the only life that has God's promise of his sustaining love and enabling power every step of the way. God's promise is the energizing concept that lifts his commands from the category of the daunting task to the realm of glorious prospect. Why? Because, as Charles Bridges has written, 'Faith in the promise gives life to the precept.'[2] God's commands, his precepts, are bound to be a great burden where there is no faith. Speaking of his unconverted pre-Christian life, the apostle Paul testified that when the precepts of God swam into his understanding, 'sin revived and I died' (Rom. 7:9). The very holiness of God's law highlighted his spiritual opposition to God, and he himself became more aware of his sinful state. Without faith, God's law came to teach him the sinfulness of sin (Rom. 7:13). After Paul had been converted to Christ, he did not cease to have struggles with sin (Rom. 7:12-25), but he knew that he was free from its guilt and condemnation, because 'the law of the Spirit of life in Christ Jesus has made me free from the law of sin and death' (Rom. 8:1-2). His new life in Christ meant that he had a new nature and his ongoing life experience of faith in Christ enabled him to receive God's commands for what they are — the Lord's powerful prescription for spiritual health and happiness! Faith sees the goal and is drawn toward it in the personal assurance that God is faithful to his promises. Once cast upon the waters of life, the 'bread' is subject to God's promise that 'after many days' we will 'find it' (11:1).

Life must be lived with commitment (11:2-5)

Bold enthusiasm marks the believer's investment in his discipleship to the Lord. To 'give a serving to seven, and also to eight' (11:2) indicates the measure of effort.

The preciousness of faith

Many people think of 'faith' as what fills the gaps left over when we can't cope on our own — a kind of mind-putty that fills the cracks we can't fix ourselves. When doctors can't cure us, or we can't figure out an answer to a problem, then we somehow can 'have faith'. 'Believing,' then, is just another option which we can exercise as need arises. Scripture, however, calls saving faith 'precious faith' (2 Peter 1:1) — a sure indication that there is nothing shallow or occasional about it. Faith in Christ is 'so precious', writes Octavious Winslow, 'that none but God can bestow it, and when bestowed it is so precious that it brings into the soul, as the queen-grace, untold blessings in its royal retinue.'* Why is this so? Winslow offers several answers:

1. Faith is precious in... (1 Peter 2:7; 2 Tim. 1:12).

2. Faith is precious in itself, because it is:
      (a) a ... of God's grace (Eph. 2:8),
      (b) the way God keeps us for... (1 Peter 1:5)
      (c) the ... of the Holy Spirit (Gal 5:22)

3. Faith is precious in ...(1 Peter 1:7)

4. Faith is precious in its fruits in our lives:
      (a) ... (Phil. 4:7)
      (b) ... (Neh. 8:10)
      (c) ... (Acts 15:9; Gal. 5:6)

*Octavious Winslow, *The Precious Things of God* (Pittsburgh: Soli Deo Gloria, 1993 [1860]), p. 66.

THINK ABOUT IT

'Seven' is symbolic of completeness. 'Eight' goes one step further — it means giving 114 per cent! The Lord Jesus Christ rose from the dead on the first day of the week, that is, on the *eighth* day. That is why Sunday is the 'Lord's Day' — the day of resurrection from the dead and of new life in Christ. It is symbolic of the New Testament age of gospel light and blessing, because Christ has brought in the 'eighth day' of new creation.[3] Giving a portion to 'eight' represents the kind of wholeheartedness that comes from a spiritual liveliness born in the heart by the Spirit of God. New life cannot but overflow (Ps. 23:5). Life lives liveliness. Life expands outward, by its very nature.

But commitment doesn't just happen. It can be dampened or fired up; it can be encouraged or inhibited. Why be wholeheartedly committed, when the world is going to be a mess whatever we do? The under-the-sun mentality can easily home in on God's men and women and tempt them to a watered-down attitude to the life and calling God has given them. Why live life with holy gusto? Why venture for the Lord? Two reasons are proposed: the first is that *time flies* (11:3-4), and the second is that we *do not need all the answers to live for God* (11:5).

1. Time flies (11:3-4)

Time and events wait for no one. Clouds full of water pour out rain; trees lie as they have fallen. We do not control these things, and so it is simply no use waiting for the ideal time or the more convenient season. If you put off living life as you ought to live it, you may find it has slipped away altogether. If the farmer sat around watching the wind and the clouds, he would neither plant nor reap. To be sure, the rain blesses the ground and gives us our food; the fallen tree provides heat for the home — the blessing of God is dropping upon the earth. That happens in his good time and according to his providence. Our responsibility is to get on with living by faith in the world as we find it. We are to trust the Lord to do his work. It is, after all, beyond our control anyway! Urgency and aggressive faith are called for and are, indeed, the channel into which God has promised to pour his blessings. Procrastination is, therefore, not only the thief of time — it is a predator upon the goodness God would give to us, were we to live committed lives for him; it is the destroyer of lives that would be filled with joy were they to receive the Lord by faith and walk in his way.

2. We do not need to know all the answers (11:5)

You do not need to understand how God works in order to find blessing in faithfulness to him (11:5). Ignorance of God's workings is not removed by having faith. God cannot be comprehended by the human mind, and it is foolishness, if not arrogance, to attempt the task. The unspoken implication is that faith in God is precisely how we can not only live with our ignorance of the secret work of God in the world, but actually find blessing in the process: 'Faith,' says Michael Eaton, 'flourishes in the mystery of providence, it does not abolish it.'[4] 'How often do we afflict and torment ourselves by our own restless thoughts,' asks John Flavel, 'when there is no real cause or ground for so doing?' Answering his own question, Flavel explains, 'How great and sure a means have the saints ever found it to their own peace, to commit all doubtful outcomes … to the Lord, and devolve all their cares upon him! "Commit thy works unto the Lord and thy thoughts shall be established" (Prov. 16:3). By works he means any doubtful, intricate, perplexing business, about which our thoughts are racked and tortured. *Roll all these upon the Lord by faith, leave them with him.*'[5]

Get on with the job (11:6)

Faith in Christ does not relieve anyone of hard work; it only makes it possible to get on with the job in a joyful spirit that expects God's blessing, whatever the immediate outcome may be. Eric Liddell, the great Christian athlete who was the hero of the Oscar-winning movie, *Chariots of Fire*, was knocked off the track while running in a 440-yard race in Stoke, England, on 14 June 1923. He refused to give up. Twenty yards down when he got back to his feet, he burned up the rain-soaked track to finish first, only to fall off the track again, this time in victorious exhaustion![6] The Preacher's counsel

WHAT THE TEXT TEACHES

is 'In the morning sow your seed, and in the evening do not withhold your hand' (11:6). Get busy! Redeem the time! Diversify your work investment by using morning and evening, even for different goals. The more doubts you have about the general situation, the more diligent you should be to get to work for the Lord in every aspect of life. If the times seem meaningless, you are called by God to bring meaning to them! If you 'sow for yourselves righteousness', then you will 'reap in [God's] mercy' (Hos. 10:12). God has promised that 'in due season we shall reap if we do not lose heart' (Gal. 6:9). Paul's encouragement to Timothy the preacher — 'be ready in season and out of season' (2 Tim. 4:2) — has its application to us all. Especially at times when we do not feel like putting in the effort ('out of season'), we should be most ceaselessly active in living life for the Lord.

The reason for such driving diligence is precisely because 'you do not know which will prosper, either this [sowing seed] or that [your evening work], or whether both alike will be good' (11:6). The point is a positive one, not a counsel of despair. We may not know the future, but God does. Our job is to work in faith and leave the rest to God. And that is where we can have a confidence that reinforces our commitment and uplifts our hearts. Our confidence is not, please note, in some mystical assurance of success in all we do; it is rather a confidence in the Lord himself and an assurance, by faith, that whatever happens, there will be a blessing in it for us. 'Those who sow in tears shall reap in joy. He who continually goes forth weeping, bearing seed for sowing, shall doubtless come again with rejoicing, bringing his sheaves with him' (Ps. 126:5-6).

QUESTIONS FOR DISCUSSION

1. Why is 'casting your bread upon the water' an act of faith (11:1)?

2. What kind of commitment does life take (11:2-6)? Why is it an urgent matter?

3. Why is it not necessary to understand how God works in order for us to be faithful?

CHAPTER
TWENTY-FOUR

LIVE
JOYFULLY!

LOOK IT UP

BIBLE READING

Ecclesiastes 11:7-10

INTRODUCTION

Christians are not called to be pious drudges. Faith is often thought of in relation to troubles: faith overcomes; faith is triumphant; faith shines from the ashes of affliction... All this is true. But faith also smiles. Joy and faith are the two sides of a gold coin. They glisten in inseparable beauty — so inseparably that it must be said that a joyless Christian is an utter contradiction. You cannot be *joyless* in the Lord if you are *in* the Lord at all. Of course life has its ebbs and flows and its ups and downs. There certainly are times of sorrow and joylessness. But it is precisely in these shifts of joy and sorrow, exultation and discouragement, that we discover all the more preciously just what the joy of the Lord means. No challenge to faith can be complete without a call to rejoice in the Lord. It was not for nothing that Paul exhorted the Philippian Christians: 'Rejoice in the Lord always. Again I will say, rejoice!' (Phil. 4:4).

Life is meant to be joyful (11:7-8)

One of the most joyful people I ever met was an old lady from Northern Ireland, long since gone to be with her Lord, who had been afflicted with crippling arthritis almost all her life. She knew she had it, when as a sixteen-year-old, she took the emigrant ship from her native land for a new life in America. Over half a century later, by then a widow with a middle-aged retarded son, she lived in a small town in Iowa. By that time she was bedridden, her limbs twisted beyond any apparent usefulness, her life restricted by pain, immobility and concern for her disabled son. The pastor, with whom I was a summer intern, prepared me for the shock of her crippling deformities, but he could never have enabled me to anticipate the sheer Christian joy radiating from that wonderful woman. Sitting at her window, a pen somehow held in her shrivelled hand, she wrote letters of encouragement to a network of Christian friends throughout the country. She was truly a fellow worker with God! Her conversation was full of life and bore testimony to a well-informed interest in the work of the Lord in the community and beyond. Above all, she was full of Christian joy and, notwithstanding her constant experience of pain and discomfort, appeared to be utterly devoid of self-pity. Her body was in ruins, but her eyes shone brightly with gospel light. She was a living testimony to the truth that a life of joy does not depend on favourable circumstances and physical well-being, but on the life of God in the soul. That joy arises from knowing the Lord Jesus Christ as a loving Saviour: it is the joy of being saved by his free grace.

1. Life is meant to be a joy (11:7)

First, rightly understood and prayerfully lived, life *in itself* is a joy: 'Truly the light is sweet, and it is pleasant for the eyes to behold the sun' (11:7). Life is, as Ernest W. Hengstenberg put it, 'a good thing; and when a gloomy and depressing mood gets the upper hand ... it is the task of the word of God to impress upon [us] this truth'.[1] All the misery of sin in the world can neither obscure this fact nor deny the experience of it to the people of God. Perhaps with a twinkle in his eye, the Preacher asks the under-the-sun sceptics if it is not pleasing to the eye 'to behold the sun'. His point is surely that the creation declares the glory of God and that it contradicts reality to assert that there is nothing but the sun under which to live. The joy inherent in sunlight — that which makes it 'sweet' — is something that speaks of God. And that voice has to be suppressed by those who do not wish to know anything of 'God who makes everything' (11:5). The Preacher's gentle barb calls the doubters and the depressed to look to the Source of the light. In gospel terms we are reminded that the 'true light' is none other than the Lord Jesus Christ (John 1:9; 8:12).

2. Joy in life is meant to last a lifetime (11:8)

Second, this joy lasts a *lifetime*. 'It's great to see the way the kids enjoy themselves ... no responsibilities,' said the woman to her friend as they walked past the playground. 'Lord knows, it'll all be over soon enough!' For many people, joy and responsibility do not mix. Children and young adults have fun, but not people with families to look after and certainly not the old and infirm. The joy that many so wistfully yearn for is the life they once knew as children, before they had any responsibility.

Yet God holds out the prospect of lifelong — and long life — blessing (Ps. 23:6; 128:5-6). 'But if a man lives many years and rejoices in them all...' does not suggest that this will be a rarity. Rather, the Lord holds out the promise of his blessing in the normal flow of life. If this was a powerful reality for Old Testament believers, how much more so it must be for New Testament Christians. Christ has brought life and immortality to light (2 Tim. 1:10). In him, there is joy enough for a whole lifetime.

3. Life is meant to be lived to the full (11:8)

Third, *realistic* reflection upon the many 'days of darkness' that will come into our lives ought to be stimulus to living life to the full now. Again, the under-the-sun perspective leaves its imprint on the Preacher's exhortation: 'All that is coming is vanity' (11:8). This is his

way of saying, 'You only have one life to live.' Everything in this (under-the-sun) life is futile, and 'fundamentally unreliable'.² He is not saying anything about either divine judgement or the world to come. He is keeping a narrow focus on this life and the motives and direction that

THINK ABOUT IT

Rejoicing as a duty

In his book *Rejoice...Always!* John Gwyn-Thomas points out that when Paul says, 'Rejoice in the Lord always. Again I say, Rejoice!' (Phil. 4:4), this 'rejoicing is laid upon us as a command; it is a duty'. He then asks, 'But how can this be a duty when rejoicing involves feeling? How can we rejoice when we do not *feel* like rejoicing?'* Can you give reasons for actually sincerely rejoicing, even when you otherwise might not feel like it? Here are some clues...

1. Paul was in prison when he wrote *Philippians.* Why did he rejoice, as in 1:18-19; 2:25,28; and 4:10.

2. Are our feelings infallible? What is the problem with so many of our feelings? Clue: Whose joy do we need in our feelings? If we lack joy, where will we find it?

3. How does God — Father, Son and Holy Spirit — give us joy? Clue: What have they done for those who believe, and what are they doing presently and for the future to secure our happiness, even in trials?

*J. Gwyn-Thomas, *Rejoice...Always!* (Edinburgh: Banner of Truth, 1989), p. 17.

we are to bring to it. We are to live and enjoy now the life God has given because it is good to do so. And, since it will soon be over, those with good sense will make the most of it. 'Why waste it,' he might have said, 'even if there is a heaven to come?' A person who refuses to live for the Lord now is not likely to live with him in glory. *Now* is the time to respond in faith to the gifts of God!

Christian joy is the real thing because it is realistic about the nature of life and death, of time and eternity, and of the holy God and sinful humanity. That realism is rooted in the revelation and redemption of God in Jesus Christ. To be saved by Christ is to know his joy — 'joy inexpressible and full of glory' (1 Peter 1:8). Claim that joy! Follow the Lord Jesus Christ.

The life of faith is full of practical joy (11:9-10)

The biblical message is always addressed to the human capacity for making choices. We are called to believe in God, to obey his will, to repent of sins, and to choose righteousness. Responsibility and the exercise of mind and will pervade the Scriptures as they do our daily lives. Perhaps surprisingly, the Bible sees joy and happiness as falling within the spectrum of volition. Enjoying life — in a biblical context, for the world's idea of *la dolce vita* is very definitely not in view — is a mandate for believers. We are to choose to live joyously! It does not just happen to us but is produced by the life of faith. This becomes clear as the writer unfolds three

fresh points as he concludes his challenge for us to invest in life.

1. Rejoice in your youth (11:9)

'Rejoice, O young man, *in your youth*' is not an invitation to sow wild oats and party into the wee small hours night after night! All of that comes naturally enough and is the dead end of under-the-sun fun and frolic, rather than the joy that pours from the fountain of eternal life. The Preacher's positive purpose is for youth to exploit its natural advantages and make a maturely happy start to life. In other words, while you are still young, you should develop to the full the gifts God has given at a time when freshness and vigour can be most productive. A misspent youth sounds like fun when told as a joke, but it is usually the precursor of a misspent adult life. Rather, be seeking true joy in all you do. All that has already been said in Ecclesiastes is packed into the Preacher's plea; all that he will say in chapter 12 will drive it home for all who have an ear to hear.

2. Rejoice in your heart (11:9)

It is *the joy of the heart* — the innermost being of a person — that is to be cultivated: 'let your heart cheer you in the days of your youth'. Says Hengstenberg, 'Cheerfulness ... is not merely permitted: it is commanded, and represented as an essential element of piety.'[3] This is the cheerfulness of heart renewed by the Spirit of God (Prov. 14:30; 15:13), not the perversity of a heart of unbelief (Num. 15:39; Jer. 17:9). When we are right with God in our hearts, then we are on track for true joy.

3. God's righteousness defines true joy (11:9)

That track is not, however, defined by the movements of our hearts and eyes. The *righteousness of God* is the standard and the ground of true joy. Joy is controlled by the awareness of God's judgement,[4] controlled in the sense that it is nurtured and developed — not restricted, as many assume. God is not a killjoy; he is the only source of lasting joy. 'Joy was created to dance with goodness, not alone.'[5]

The kind of joy you seek now will go a long way to determining what fruit will be produced in later life. An old term for the down side of wasted youth is *after-wretchedness* — the sad ruination of middle and later life that resulted from earlier follies.

Perhaps the opposite ought to be called *after-joy* — the joy that grows by God's grace in Jesus Christ after a sinner is saved and at whatever age he is saved. The Preacher wants that blessing to begin early in people's lives. Therefore, he calls us to remove the obstacles to a fruitful and happy life. 'Remove sorrow' and 'put away evil from your flesh', for 'childhood and youth are vanity' (11:10). The under-the-sun motif appears again, for he seems to be warning against not only the pitfalls of sin in the heart and in the flesh, but also the false trust in youth and vigour that is so common in our culture. 'Youth' as an abstraction — a golden age of life

— is dangerously meaningless. The cult of youth-fulness is a broken reed. The agelessness of J. M. Barrie's Peter Pan is as much of a fantasy as Tinkerbell, the fairy in the story. Youth is a quickly passing phase. It can be a time of joy — in the Lord. But under-the-sun youth is a secular mirage that must crumble into joyless regret as advancing time erodes the porcelain finish of the beauty shop and opens up the fissures of irreversible decay. To trust in such youth is to trust in the illusions of the make-up artist. It is to embalm an abstraction and imagine it to be reality.

Invest in life! Cast your bread upon the waters of your times! The Preacher challenges us to pour our hearts into a faith-response to God's gift of life. It only remains for him to face us with the final challenge: to come to know our Creator as our own Saviour and Lord. And that is the subject of his final chapter.

QUESTIONS FOR DISCUSSION

1. *Is life supposed to be sad and miserably difficult (11:7-8)?*

2. *How is joy to be obtained in practice (11:9-10)?*

3. *Discuss the purpose of God for youth and some of the pitfalls of a youthfulness that is not dedicated to the Lord.*

CHAPTER
TWENTY-FIVE

REMEMBER YOUR CREATOR!

LOOK IT UP

BIBLE READING

Ecclesiastes 12:1-7

INTRODUCTION

The final chapter is the climax of the Preacher's appeal. He calls for decision and commitment. And the heart of that commitment is not the anticipation of comprehensive inside information about God's plans and providence; neither is it the expectation of a happy life unencumbered by the problems that drop into everybody else's horizon; it is the remembering of God for who he is — the Creator-God who has made us and placed us in the real world, so that we would be his people in thought, word and deed. It is knowing *him* … personally and with confiding trust and expectant love. We are called to 'fear God and keep his commandments, for this is the whole duty of man' (12:13, NIV). This is the subject of the climactic challenge of Ecclesiastes.

Remember (12:1)

Remembering things can be a real problem sometimes. A particularly gifted preacher who has a masterly command of language tells that ever since the day he forgot the Lord's Prayer in the middle of leading his congregation in its recitation, he has never gone into the pulpit without a written copy as back-up for his memory! A momentary mental lapse can suddenly produce a blank in the most richly furnished of memories!

The meaning of 'forgetting' in the Bible is, however, a different kind of animal altogether! Forgetting God was the great failing of God's people in the Old Testament period (Deut. 32:18; Isa. 17:10; 51:13). Indeed, 'all the nations that forget God' fall under the cloud of his righteous anger (Ps. 9:17). And this is no mere mental lapse on their part, but a determined attitude of heart. It is a *commitment* to forget the Lord, by laying his word and his will to one side. Forgetting the Lord is the other side of living for self. It is part of the Christless, unconverted lifestyle; the instinctive revulsion from the light and impulsion toward the darkness; the unwillingness to receive the things that come from the Spirit of God; the rejection of the knowledge of God and the willing acceptance of what the Lord has declared to be sin (John 3:19; 1 Cor. 2:14; Rom. 1:28,32).

Remembering the Lord is, likewise, a good deal more than merely sparing him a thought. When the Lord's people were exiled in Babylon, they confessed their faith-remembrance of God in the most profound language of personal devotion. 'If I forget you, O Jerusalem, let my right hand forget its skill. If I do not remember you, let my tongue cling to the roof of my mouth — if I do not exalt Jerusalem above my chief joy' (Ps. 137:5-6). At the heart of this longing for Jerusalem is not the place itself, but the person of the living God, who has made an everlasting covenant with his people, that they would be his adopted children and he their heavenly Father. In him there is life, and apart from him there is nothing. To forget him is to be in the state of spiritual death. To remember him is to know life and to have it abundantly. Jerusalem is the fountain of his free grace because there, in the temple, God was present with his people and making provision for their redemption. Yet all this only pointed to Jesus Christ, who was both temple and sacrifice, both great high priest and blood of atonement, both mediator and sin-bearer on behalf of his people. To long for Jerusalem was to desire all that it represented: for salvation, yes, but all the more for union and communion with the only Saviour of sinners. If your heart has been renewed by the transforming action of the Holy Spirit, and your life turned around through radical repentance and faith in Christ as the only Saviour from sin, then how can you not be powerfully drawn to remember all that the Lord has done in pouring out undeserved goodness upon you. The believer remembers because he loves: 'I love the LORD, because he has heard my voice and my supplications. Because he has inclined his ear to me, therefore I will call upon him as long as I live... Gracious is the LORD, and righteous; yes, our God is merciful. The LORD preserves the simple; I was brought low, and he saved me' (Ps. 116:1-2,5-6).

What is precious to a believer must become as precious to the person who as yet has not trusted in the Lord. The Preacher was speaking to the community of God's covenant people, Israel. They knew the message of God's Word, even if they were largely ignoring its claims. But that is just the point! The thrust of Solomon's words is directed to the *unbelief* among God's people. It therefore strikes toward the need of all human beings, whether they hear God's Word for the first or the umpteenth time. Those who are oppressed by the meaninglessness of life under the sun and see the emptiness of their lives need desperately to remember the only one who can redeem such a lost state and fill up the caverns of our despair with his everlasting love! The Preacher outlines the three basic motives for remembering the Lord.

1. You owe it to your Creator! (12:1)

Remember your Creator! The Hebrew *boreka* ('Creator') is a plural form, no doubt echoing the language of Genesis 1:26: 'Let us make man in *our* image, according to *our* likeness.' This is an indication of the greatness of God's majesty, as Michael Eaton has suggested [1] but also, surely, an intimation of the three-in-one glory of God the Father, Son and Holy Spirit. The connection is then made — to be sure, only in the light of New Testament hindsight — between the first creation of man as the image-bearer of God and the new creation

'Ho Everyone that Thirsteth'*

1. The poet A. E. Housman reflects on the evanescence of youth and its illicit pleasures, and seems to see no alternative to living under the sun and indulging the flesh before it is too late.

> Ho, everyone that thirsteth
>   And hath the price to give,
> Come to the stolen waters,
>   Drink and your soul shall live.
>
> Come to the stolen waters
>   And leap the guarded pale,
> And pull the flower in season
>   Before desire shall fail.
>
> It shall not last forever,
>   No more than earth and skies;
> But he that drinks in season
>   Shall live before he dies.
>
> June suns, you cannot store them
>   To warm the winter's cold,
> The lad that hopes for heaven
>   Shall fill his mouth with mould.

2. Notice how Houseman uses allusions to Isaiah 55:1, John 7:37, and Ecclesiastes 12:5. Note also that whereas the poet's lad ends his existence in the grave after his 'under the sun' life, Solomon's youth is urged to live today out of the eternity that he must soon enter. He points us to the salvation and the hope of heaven that Houseman dismally dismisses as utter illusion.

* F Kermode and J. Hollander, *The Oxford Anthology of English Literature* (London: Oxford University Press, 1973), 2:2035.

THINK ABOUT IT

in God's only-begotten Son, the Lord Jesus Christ, of all who will believe on him in this world.

This effectively implies that God is entitled to be remembered by those whom he has made. He has the exclusive rights to your worship, service and discipleship! The potter has power over the clay. Not only can you not rightly talk back to God, but you are under an unbreakable obligation to confess him as Lord (Rom. 9:20-21)! You owe this to our Creator. You have no right to forget him and go your own way!

2. You owe it to yourself ... now (12:1)

Remember the Lord 'in the days of your youth'. Some people think that youth is a time for enjoying an almost deliberate irresponsibility. It is taken for granted that young people will sow their wild oats. Such an attitude is a self-fulfilling prophecy, and the only trouble with it is the crop failure that inevitably follows! We reap as we sow, and wasted youth may be no better than a jolly fun-filled foretaste of a miserable middle age. When Israel journeyed through the Sinai desert *en route* for Canaan, they were promised their food, in the form of manna they could collect each day except the Sabbath (Exod. 16:4-5,19-23). The manna did not, however, collect itself: the Lord's people had to get up early and gather it in. They had to collect it before it rotted. Laziness was bad for manna! Youth is like this: if you want a fruitful life (manna), then 'let the manna be gathered early in the day'.² Start young! Look at the barren sadness of many in middle and old age, and ask

yourself what you are building for your future now. You will reap later what you sow now — either for good or for ill. Your potential calls you into God's future for your life. Now is the time to begin to realize that potential for your blessing. Your youth is prime time in God's eyes: a time for responsibility, for learning the things that are really important, for moulding God-honouring patterns of life; a time for sowing in righteousness in the Lord and experiencing the fruit that Jesus spoke of in the parable of the sower: 'some a hundredfold, some sixty, some thirty' (Matt. 13:23).

God wants the energy, liveliness, imagination, freshness and eager expectancy of youth and to spread the light of the good news of Christ into every nook and cranny of the next generation as it takes its place in the forefront of societal and cultural development. You owe it to yourself, under God, to take his outstretched hand and, in dependence upon his grace, to realize the fulness of the calling to which he has called you in the gospel of Jesus Christ. Should you not want God's best for your life?

3. You owe it to your future (12:1)

Commit yourself to the Lord 'before the difficult days come, and the years draw near when you say, "I have no pleasure in them"'. Again, there are echoes here of the Genesis account of human origins — not creation itself, but rather the fall of man into sin and its terrible consequences. Because of sin, we all return to the dust (Gen. 3:19). Like some black-draped Victorian hearse from a Gothic horror story, Death is preceded by footmen called Infirmity and Old Age, whose appearance is a foretaste of the end that must come soon for all living.

The Preacher's intention is not to titillate our morbid fantasies, still less to plunge us into a gloomy frame of mind, but rather to encourage us to anticipate the future and its trials realistically and be in the spiritual condition to face them head-on and win. Summer is the time to prepare for winter, and old age is our physical winter. It can also be a devastating spiritual winter if our hearts are unprepared. Charles Bridges pinpoints the issue: 'Old age, with all its train and retinue of weakness and infirmities, will come. But if it *bends your back*, do not keep your sins to *break it.*'[3] Life does *not* get any easier. And it is no more than cruel mockery to tell people in the twilight of life, 'Pack up your troubles in your old kit-bag and smile, smile, smile,' when what is really needed is the solid bedrock of unshakeable personal faith in the risen, life-giving Saviour. As the outward man crumbles away, the inner person needs more than a party hat and the illusion of youth and beauty!

The apostle Paul opens up God's answer for us in 2 Corinthians 4:16 - 6:2. This passage is required reading for a proper understanding of Ecclesiastes 12. Paul could see the decline of his physical faculties. Outwardly he was 'perishing'. There was no use denying it

WHAT THE TEXT TEACHES

— our bodies are declining assets. But, says Paul, 'we do not lose heart'. Why? Because 'the inward man is being renewed day by day' (4:16). His eyes were fixed on the unseen eternal glory he was receiving in Jesus Christ, rather than on his very visible aches, pains and ageing. In a ringing affirmation of the truth that really counts, Paul declares, 'For we know that if our earthly house, this tent, is destroyed, we have a building from God, a house not made with hands, eternal in the heavens' (5:1). The Christian prepares for the future by living out of the future; he lives each day in terms of the unfolding toward him of God's perfect purpose for his future. Faith and confidence go hand in hand. And the Christian owes it to the future to which God is calling him to live now for his Father-God the life of the kingdom of heaven, on this side of eternity!

Reflect (12:2-7)

The thought that years will come when we will say, 'I have no pleasure in them' (12:1), is as disturbing as it is unappealing. Cornelis Gilhuis relates how, while visiting a parishioner who had just turned eighty-five, the venerable old man suddenly said to him, 'Above my life I could now write the words: "No more".' His wife and friends were dead. His house, health and hearing were gone. He lived in an old people's home, and so his freedom was restricted. He could not walk very well, anyway. And his memory was slipping too. So much he had known and enjoyed was … no more. Eventually he too would be … no more.[4]

This is what the Preacher reflects upon in the highly poetic language of Ecclesiastes 12. Through the successive phases of the advance of sorrows, the decline of physical capacities, and death itself, the author takes us to the threshold of decision — the urgency of rejecting the meaninglessness of an 'under the sun' death-wish society by remembering the Lord of life. The poetic wistfulness with which he explores the facts while masking something of their harshness is a lesson in itself. This is how to preach the good news through breaking the bad news! Cast in figurative language, the bad news is raised from the baldly horrific, earthy facts of decay and death to an altogether higher plane. The Preacher's elevated language takes us from the cold slab of the mortuary to the quietness of the secret place of meditation, prayer and the worship of God. We are brought to the loftier consideration that what is lost through physical decline is not some mere phase, or the perception of a phase, in a normal under-the-sun cycle of human existence that grinds on, only to end with a dull thud as 'another one bites the dust!' Rather, the author's transition from the merely prosaic into the poetic commands our thoughtful reflection and suggests that there is something better than decline and death. Let us rather see this life, warts and all, as God's chosen arena in which he is working to change our lives and bring spiritual fruitfulness even against the

background of physical incapacity. God is saying that the inevitable need not be the ultimate! Now, in youth, and later, in old age, God will produce in all his worshipping people nothing less than the beauty of his holiness — new life redeemed from death by his free grace in his own dear Son, Jesus Christ!

1. Reflect on advancing sorrows (12:2)

The sun, light, moon and stars grow dark. Rain ceases, only for clouds to return. Real life is a darkling landscape. Sorrows multiply and hearts grow heavier. Grey days make for furrowed brows. The point is that if anyone is to be encouraged and cheered in his old age, that spiritual uplift will have to come from outside his personal resources. The perfect illustration is the famous description of Scottish weather. If you can see the hills, it's going to rain; if you can't see the hills, it *is* raining. Old age is a bit like the Scottish climate: there are many rainy days. And joy will vanish with the sun, if it is not born from and firmly rooted in knowing the Lord through a living faith. Remember your Creator in the days of your youth!

2. Reflect on declining faculties (12:3-5)

The proof that the clock cannot be turned back is found in everything we take for granted when we are young:

a. The 'keepers of the house' are the hands and arms that shake and lose their strength where once they worked indefatigably (v. 3).

b. The 'strong men' are the legs that are now bent and pad along the street with shortened stride and unsteady gait (v. 3).

c. The 'grinders' are the teeth long lost to dentures and the painful bite of wasted gums (v. 3).

d. Those that 'look through the windows' are the eyes, now dimmed, in spite of glasses, so that reading and even general vision offer little pleasure (v. 3).

e. The 'doors … in the street' are the ears that hear no more with the clarity of earlier days (v. 4).

f. The 'sound of the grinding' is a voice, once strong, that has faded to a whisper (v. 4).

g. To 'rise up at the sound of a bird' while 'all the daughters of music are brought low' is a reference to the light sleep and early waking of the aged, without the consolation of being able to enjoy the dawn chorus of the singing birds (v. 4).

h. Being 'afraid of height' is that loss of a sure foot and steady balance that makes stairs a trial to the old (v. 5).

i. The 'terrors in the way' can range from children on bikes to fast cars and muggers who prey on the infirm. The great world outside holds threats that once never crossed a man's mind (v. 5).

j. The blossoming of the 'almond tree' is hair turning grey and then white — beautiful in itself, but only for a moment — for, just as the petals drop within a few days, so the greying of the hair marks the fleeting passage of our life (v. 5).

k. The 'grasshopper is a burden' conjures up the image of a late autumn day, with a tired old grasshopper — a survivor of the summer — crawling slowly across our doorstep, his joints too stiff to give free movement to his legs, his muscles too cold and emaciated to speed him on his weary way (v. 5).

l. Then 'desire fails': the general appetite for life, for food, for anything in the spectrum of experience, recedes, and no vitamins or drugs can rekindle the former fires of youthful *joie de vivre* (v. 5).[5]

And then comes death...

3. Reflect on death (12:5)

'For man goes to his eternal home, and the mourners go about the streets.' Nothing is said here of eternity or life after death. The 'eternal home' is simply the grave. The central idea is that this life, once over, is gone for ever — there is no return, no reincarnation, no bringing back to life by cryonic technology.[6] Life is a one-way trip. Mention of mourners bathes the scene in unutterable sadness. Dying is a palpable outrage. It is the violation of something that is good in its very nature — the gift of life. Indeed, the Hebrew text reads, 'Man *is going* to his eternal home': the participle (Heb., *holekh*) underlines the ongoing nature of the process.[7] We are dying while we live. Where, in this, can meaning be found? Reflect ... and 'remember'.

Now is the time to remember (12:6-7)

The Preacher pictures for us a golden lamp bowl suspended on a silver chain and a pitcher at a well, raised and lowered by a wheel. Such things decay: the light goes out, the pitcher can draw water no more. The time to use them to the full is now! And so it is with life itself. Like silver and gold, like water from a well, life is precious and time is a gift of grace to be invested for a harvest of fulfilment and of service under God.

Soon your 'dust will return to the earth as it was, and the spirit will return to God who gave it' (12:7). Why were you given life? To bring glory to the Lord by living as his image-bearer in your life on earth. How are you living your life? And when he calls your spirit into his presence, what will your testimony be as to that life?

For whom are you living? What are your goals? Who is your god? Where are you going? The time for decision is now — the unuttered implication of the Preacher's word is that a mistake now may be a mistake for ever! 'Remember him ... before ... before...' (12:6).

DISCUSS IT

1. Define 'forgetting' as used in Deuteronomy 32:18; Isaiah 17:10; and 51:13.

2. What does it mean to 'remember' the Lord (see Ps. 137:5-6). And why are we to remember the Lord (12:1)?

3. Do you think it is morbid to reflect on old age and death (12:2-8)? List the details of this passage and state why they encourage us to remember the Lord.

CHAPTER
TWENTY-SIX

TIME TO
RESPOND!

BIBLE READING

Ecclesiastes 12:8-14

The Preacher has turned full circle. He returns to his first words: "'Vanity of vanities!" says the Preacher. "All is vanity!'" (12:8; cf. 1:1). Like every good preacher, he concludes with his text! It is his way of saying to us: How have I treated my subject? Have I kept to the text? Have I opened its meaning clearly? Have I spoken to your heart? Have I illuminated the problem? Have I pointed to the solution? Have you thought it through with me? Are you ready to respond?

The purpose of Ecclesiastes, says J. I. Packer, is to lead a 'young believer into true wisdom'.[1] This is not the same thing, however, as having answers to all the questions and puzzles of life. Packer illustrates this by contrasting the view from the platform at York Railway Station with that of the electronic display in the 'signal box' between Platforms 7 and 8. On the platform, your view of approaching trains is rather limited, but up above, in the control centre, moving lights map the trains for miles around. Packer's point is that some Christians think of the wisdom of

God, and their experience of knowing God, according to this latter model. They feel they ought to be like the man in the signal box and have a comprehensive understanding of all of life's mysteries and challenges; that to have the wisdom of God is to be able to 'discern the real purpose of everything that happens to them' and to be clear at 'every moment how God was making all things work together for good'.[2] But the mistake, Packer says, is 'to equate wisdom with wide knowledge', whereas what we need to learn is that 'the real basis of wisdom is a frank acknowledgement that this world's course is enigmatic, that much of what happens is quite inexplicable to us, and that most occurrences "under-the-sun" bear no outward sign of a rational, moral God ordering them at all'.[3] The fact is, that God does not let Christians in on his secret councils; we are still on the platform with everybody else.

The difference is that God's people have been given a faith that is real and a realism that is faithful. Even our ignorance is, by God's grace, made the occasion of working in us a genuine humility and a dependence upon God's goodness in his unseen purposes. God's way of wisdom for us is not some mystical divining of his secret will. It is the way of personal commitment and lively faith whereby we can 'trust him and rejoice in him, even when we cannot discern his path'.[4] Solomon now makes three vital points, our response to which will make the difference between life and death, and therefore meaning and meaninglessness. Basically he says, this is *the truth*, it is the *only truth* and this is the *most urgent truth!*

It is truth! (12:9-10)

For one thing, you have been told the truth. The
Preacher declares that all he has said is 'upright
— words of truth' (12:10). He has clearly exposed
the true meaninglessness of under-the-sun secularism. He has exercised all the skill and wisdom at his command. He knows he is wise, a
good communicator, a wordsmith of proverbs,
and a minister of truth. Yet for all the authority
with which he speaks, there is almost a pleading tone in the way he appeals to his readers. It
has been no academic exercise, but an explanation of the issues of life and death, of meaning
and of emptiness, of the realities of time and eternity. It has been a *Word from God!*

It is the only truth! (12:11-12)

Furthermore, don't accept any substitutes! Why?
Because whoever was given to set out the Word
of God, the actual source is the 'one Shepherd'
— the same Shepherd as in Psalm 23, namely,
Jehovah, the God of Israel. The metaphors of
these words as 'goads' and 'well-driven nails'
emphasizes their transcendent authority and
transforming power. The excellent Edward
Reynolds comments, 'Hereby then is noted, the
divine authority of the Holy Scriptures, delivered
by inspiration to the penmen thereof for the use

of the church; the spirit of Christ being in those that wrote them (1 Peter 1:11; 2 Peter 1:21; 2 Tim. 3:16; 2 Cor. 13:3; Heb. 1:1-2)' (Reynolds: 254).

The intimate connection, in verse 12, of an encouragement to 'be admonished by these' [words from God] and a discouragement from becoming bogged down in the study of the books and discourses that flow endlessly from other sources, serves to underline the uniqueness of the Word of God. This is not an anti-intellectualist book-burning spirit, but a realistic perspective on the limitations, not to say dangers, of a great deal of so-called scholarship.

It is urgent truth! (12:13-14)

When Solomon says, 'Let us hear the conclusion of the whole matter,' it is, as Bishop Reynolds says, 'an exordium [an introduction preparing for what follows] to stir up attention' (Reynolds: 256); that is, he is shouting a loud 'Hear this!' This is the point to which everything has been leading! So pay attention and don't miss it. You have come this far. Don't fall at the last hurdle.

This 'conclusion' comprises a double point. One concerns the Lord and the other his Word. These are the twin foci of the entire book: 'Fear God and keep his commandments, for this is the whole duty of man' (12:13, NIV). This rather stark statement, to which is added an ominous intimation of the final judgement of God on everything, whether good or evil (12:14), comes as something of a cold shock. And yet it is the whole

Why people don't become Christians

Asahel Nettleton (1783-1844) was perhaps the greatest preacher of the Second Great Awakening in North America. Thousands were saved under his ministry. In a message on Luke 13:24, he powerfully sets out the reasons why many who hear the gospel decide to stay lost.

1. They do not seek salvation as a thing of first importance (Matt. 6:33; 13:44).
2. They seek salvation through their own righteousness (Luke 18:11-12; Rom. 10:3).
3. They take attitudes that prevent their preparation for heaven: they can't see a need to be regenerated in their hearts (John 3:3,5,7); or a need for repentance (Matt. 7:13; cf. John 10:1).
4. They do not seek Christ at the right time (Matt. 25:11-12; Luke 13:25-27; Heb. 12:16-17).
5. They are not willing to part with everything in order to have heaven (Luke 18:18-23; cf. Luke 9:23,61-62).
6. 'Some seek for a time and then drop the subject' (John 6:66).

Do **you** understand the urgency of coming to Jesus Christ for salvation? Do you understand that the gospel call is **a call** and not an 'option' to be taken up if and when you feel like it?

But hear the Saviour's word:
'Strive for the heavenly gate'.
Many will call upon the Lord,
And find their cries too late.*

* Asahel Nettleton, *The Door is Open* (Darlington: Evangelical Press, 1998), 40 pages. Get a copy of this booklet, read it, study it — and look to Jesus Christ as your Saviour and Lord.

THINK ABOUT IT

point! It can be unpacked into some leading questions that challenge the conscience to the depths.

1. Do you know God?
2. Are you keeping his commandments?
3. Have you acknowledged your accountability before him?
4. Will you confess that God is just in all his judgements?

Outside of God and a loving reverence for him and his revealed will, there really can only be vanity and meaninglessness! The full revelation of the New Testament now clothes this truth with the evangelical warmth of the gospel of Christ. The apostle John tells New Testament believers: 'Beloved, if our heart does not condemn us, we have confidence toward God. And whatever we ask we receive from him, because we keep his commandments and do those things that are pleasing in his sight. *And this is his commandment: that we should believe on the name of his Son, Jesus Christ and love one another, as he gave us commandment.* Now he who keeps his commandments abides in him, and he in him. And by this we know that he abides in us, by the Spirit he has given us' (1 John 3:21-24). God has revealed himself to us in all his fulness as the Three-in-One, full of love and grace; the Father-God who is love and is to be worshipped in holy fear; the incarnate Son, the Lord Jesus Christ, the mediator who has died in our place to bear our sins; and the Holy Spirit, who since Pentecost has ministered in the hearts of God's people with transforming power.

A time for personal commitment

On 20 May 1962, a seventeen-year-old lad joined his pals from his school Scripture Union group for a day trip to Galashiels, a small town in the southern uplands of Scotland. The business of that beautiful spring day was a five-a-side soccer tournament followed by a picnic and an evening gospel rally. Hundreds of young people gathered from all over the south-east of Scotland for this annual event. The soccer was pretty ferocious that afternoon, and it was a weary young fellow who settled into his seat at the meeting, his mind reverberating with the chagrin of a narrow defeat in the quarter-final and wondering if he could really be bothered with a sermon on a Saturday night. But you never know, he said to himself, the preacher might bring a good message.

The preacher was a Mr Gordon, a minister from over the border in Newcastle-upon-Tyne. He opened his Bible and read from the book of Ecclesiastes, chapter 12. As he thundered out the message of that text, line upon line and precept upon precept — always pointing to its thrust in the light of the New Testament fulness of the gospel of Jesus Christ — that teenage audience slid forward to the edge of the hard wooden benches of the Volunteer Hall. As the fleeting gift of youth was set in the context of a short life and a long eternity, the tiredness of limb and mind fled from that seventeen-year-old. He began to hold his breath as the issues of life and death coursed through his head with relentless impetus. He saw, as never before, how life was a gift so easily wasted, how even that day he had been more interested in the soccer than in the Saviour. For the first time in his life, he saw, with awesome reality, that he was neither right with God nor committed to his Son, as he had lightly imagined from childhood. He felt suspended between life and death, between self and Christ, between his sins and the Saviour; and he knew he was being drawn inexorably to the moment of decision — he must choose that day whom he would serve!

Going home that night, he watched the cat's-eyes along the central median of the A68 sparkling in the headlights of the bus. Ahead of them, the road wound through unseen darkness to his home in Edinburgh. The lights seemed, however, to chart a new path for a new life in Jesus Christ. Life would never be the same again. Christ had come and saved him to be his disciple. Christ had brought him by his free grace to remember his Creator in the days of his youth. Christ, he saw, was the only true meaning in an otherwise lost and meaningless under-the-sun world. And Christ had died on that cross so long ago to bring redemption to the likes of him!

I was that young lad. Forty years on, I can surely say that my life has never been the same again. But throughout the passages of life, the Lord Jesus Christ has been the unchanging Saviour and the ever faithful Friend. He is the meaning of our life! He is Immanuel — 'God-with-us' — and in him we can have life and have it abundantly! Then we declare with a full heart, 'O God, you have taught me from my youth; and to this day I declare your wondrous works' (Ps. 71:17).

QUESTIONS FOR DISCUSSION

1. *Discuss each numbered point in the 'Think about...' box. What is your personal attitude to each of these?*

2. *What response is the Lord looking for from each one of us (12:8-14)? What kind of life does he have in store for those who heed his call?*

3. *Write out a statement of your personal commitment to Jesus Christ. Be honest about your lack of commitment and list some practical matters in which you promise to change your ways.*

NOTES

Introduction

1. Malcolm Muggeridge has pinpointed this with his characteristic blend of wit and acerbity in an illuminating essay, 'The true crisis of Our Time', in Geoffrey Barlow, ed. *Vintage Muggeridge* (Grand Rapids: Eerdmans, 1985). He says that 'in the gadarene bias apparent in all our policies and projects ... we are confronted, not with a whole series of crises and problems, but with one crisis amounting to a death wish, an urge to self-destruction seeping into every aspect of our way of life, especially our values, our belief, our aspirations, how we see the past and our hopes for the future' (p.101).
2. Francis A. Schaeffer, *Death in the City* (London: Inter-Varsity, 1969), p.20.
3. General Millan Astray uttered these astonishing words in Seville, on 15 August 1936. The Spanish Civil War was raging and the General, whose martial exploits had left him with one leg, one arm, one eye, and only a few fingers on his remaining hand, was completely carried away by his own rhetoric — not uninfluenced, perhaps, by his own remarkable survival from the rigours of his profession. See Hugh Thomas, *The Spanish Civil War* (New York: Harper and Row, 1963), pp.271-72.
4. Alan Richardson, *Christian Apologetics* (London: SCM, 1963), p.29.
5. Michael Eaton, *Ecclesiastes*, Tyndale Old Testament Commentaries (Leicester: Inter-Varsity, 1983), p.47.

Chapter 1: What's the use?

1. Shelley's fictional king, Ozymandius, was the historical Rameses II. His 'shattered visage' is in remarkably good shape and on display in the British Museum, London.

See F. Kermode and J. Hollander, The *Oxford Anthology of English Literature*, vol.2 (London: Oxford University Press, 1973), p.414.

2. The identity of the 'Preacher' (Heb. *Qoheleth*) is one of the great conundrums of biblical interpretation. He would appear to be Solomon (1:1,12; 12:9). See C. Bridges, *Ecclesiastes*, pp. vii-viii, for a clear defence of this position. It is more fashionable these days to see Ecclesiastes as the work of an unknown author who has melded materials of his own and others, including material of Solomonic authorship, and attributed them to a 'Preacher', who is a personification of Solomonic-style wisdom. (See Herbert C. Leupold, *Exposition of Ecclesiastes* [Grand Rapids: Baker, 1972 (1952)], pp.8-17; and Eaton, *Ecclesiastes*, pp.21-24, for discussions of the issues involved.)

3. Many commentators argue that the conditions in Solomon's time (see 1 Kings 4:20,24) do not mesh with the Preacher's picture of the sad state of Israel and hold that Ecclesiastes is contemporaneous with Malachi, with a post-exilic provenance and purpose. A straightforward reading of the book, however, reveals the conditions of many an ancient kingdom at the height of its glory. Is there, for instance, no poverty, oppression or despair in the wealthiest and most powerful nations in our world? Such an argument against Solomonic authorship is contrived, to say the least. (See Leupold, *Ecclesiastes*, p.12.)

4. R. Laird Harris *et al.*, *Theological Wordbook of the Old Testament*, vol.1 (Chicago: Moody, 1980), pp.204-5.

5. Douglas R. Groothuis, *Unmasking the New Age* (Downers Grove, Ill: Inter-Varsity, 1986), pp.52-55.

Groothuis shows how the New Age mysticism is 'a cosmic humanism' in which all meaning is found in 'the One' as man absorbs God's functions and creation becomes a mystical continuum of existence. When the Creator-creature distinction is obliterated, the creature becomes his own god and is the source of his own ultimate meaning. The facts of his existence, however, are an embarrassing reminder, from time to time, of his true creaturehood. The gnawing awareness of futility can never quite be drowned out, however loud the protestation of man's new independence of God.

Chapter 2: Three facts of life

1. Erich Maria Remarque, *All Quiet on the Western Front* (New York: Grosset and Dunlap, 1929), p.278. This classic antiwar novel speaks, of course, of the experience of soldiers in the trenches of World War 1. The theme, however, is a statement of meaning in a secular world. Paul Baumer, the ill-fated hero, is modern man, stripped of the delusions of childhood (and, by implication, of religion). 'I am young,' he says, 'I am twenty years old; yet I know nothing of life but despair, death, fear and fatuous superficiality cast over an abyss of sorrow' (see pp.270ff.).
2. Davin Seay, *Stairway to Heaven* (New York: Ballantine, 1986), p.171. This is an illuminating survey of 'the spiritual roots of rock 'n' roll from the King and Little Richard to Prince and Amy Grant'.

Chapter 3: Knowledge numbs

1. Derek Kidner, *A Time to Mourn, and a Time to Dance* (Leicester: Inter-Varsity, 1976), p.29.
2. Hymn 637 in *The Church Hymnary* (London: Oxford University Press, 1930).
3. Herbert C. Leupold, *Exposition of Ecclesiastes* (Grand Rapids: Baker, 1972 [1952]), p.56.

Chapter 4: Pleasure palls

1. Robert Ingram, 'Multiplying by Zero', in *Tabletalk,* vol.11, no.4 (August 1987), p.6.
2. Gordon H. Clark, *From Thales to Dewey — A History of Philosophy* (Grand Rapids: Baker, 1980 [1957]), p.151. The founder of the Cyrenaics was Aristippus of Cyrene (435-366 B.C.). Epicurus of Samos (341-270 B.C.) founded the school that bore his name.
3. Francis Nigel Lee, *A Christian Introduction to the History of Philosophy* Nutley, N.J.: Craig Press, 1969, p.88.
4. Eaton, *Ecclesiastes,* p.65.
5. The moderate use of wine is a recurring thought in the Wisdom literature (Eccles. 9:9; Prov. 31:6-7). There is no suggestion that excessive drinking — or, say (in the modern idiom), the use of drugs, is an aid to thinking and the development of human potential in some mind-altering way.
6. In 1811 John Knill of St Ives in England built a pyramid like a church steeple inscribed with the text, 'I know that my Redeemer liveth' (Job 19:25). After his death he left an endowment and directions that every five years, ten young girls in white should dance around the 'folly' and sing the one hundredth psalm ('All people that on earth do dwell') in his memory. This is observed in St Ives to this day, to the evident pleasure of locals and tourists alike. England, particularly, abounds in such cultural curiosities.
7. Kidner, *A Time,* p.32.

Chapter 5: Who's in charge?

1. William E. Henley, 'Invictus', in *A Treasury of the World's Best Loved Poets* (New York: Avanel Books, 1980), p.122.

2. Ernest W. Hengstenberg, *A Commentary on Ecclesiastes* (Minneapolis: James and Klock, 1977 [1869]), p.92, quotes extensively from Luther.
3. Eaton, *Ecclesiastes,* pp.79-80.
4. Leupold, *Ecclesiastes*, p.85.

Chapter 6: Eternity in your heart
1. Hengstenberg, *Ecclesiastes*, pp.104-5.
2. Augustine, *Confessions,* 1.1.
3. Hengstenberg, *Ecclesiastes*, p.121.

Chapter 7: Empty lives
1. Charles Bridges, *Ecclesiastes* (Edinburgh: Banner of Truth, 1981 [1860]), p.79.
2. Christian Solidarity International (CSI) has published a world map with a cross entangled with barbed wire superimposed on each country in which state restriction or proscription of Christian work and witness is known to be operative (Christian Solidarity International, Box 24042, Washington, D.C. 20024).
3. Herbert Schlossberg, *Idols for Destruction* (Nashville: Thomas Nelson, 1983). See pp.59-74 for a challenging review of current concepts of poverty and its cure.

Chapter 8: The rat race
1. Tony Walter, *All You Love is Need* (London: SPCK, 1985), p.39.
2. Ibid., p.125.
3. Bridges, *Ecclesiastes,* p.87.
4. Kidner, *A Time*, p.46.
5. Ibid., p.52.
6. Leupold, *Ecclesiastes*, p.115.
7. Kidner, *A Time*, p.52.

Chapter 9: Hollow religion
1. James Barke, ed., *Poems and Songs of Robert Burns* (London

and Glasgow: Collins, 1969), pp. 105ff. The poem, 'The Cottar's Saturday Night', is thought to be an evocation of Burns's childhood. Like so many prodigals before and since, Burns had a genuine love and wistful respect for godly parents.

2. Herbert Schlossberg, *Idols*, pp. 232ff. In a chapter entitled 'Idols of Religion', the author traces the relationship of church to society in America, noting its parallels with the kind of apostasy described in the Old Testament, particularly in the prophets such as Isaiah. His focus is on the tendency toward 'civil religion' that accommodates the cultural norms of a practically godless society. The Preacher, as we have noted, focuses on the individual's spiritual experience as he relates personally to God.

3. Leupold, *Ecclesiastes,* p.117.

4. Kidner, *A Time*, p.52.

5. W. H. Gispen, *Exodus*, Bible Student's Commentary (Grand Rapids: Zondervan/Paideia, 1982), p.52.

6. Eaton, *Ecclesiastes*, p.97. H. C. Leupold (*Ecclesiastes*, p.118) thinks only the temple is in view.

7. Robert Leighton, *Commentary on First Peter* (Grand Rapids: Kregel, 1972), p.291. Robert Leighton (1611-84) was the Archbishop of Glasgow, Scotland, during the period of the Stuart Restoration. His First Peter commentary is one of the classics of biblical exposition.

Chapter 10: Promises to keep

1. Reformed Presbyterian Church, *The Constitution of the Reformed Presbyterian Church of North America* (Pittsburgh: 1989), p. GA.

2. Samuel Nesdoly, *Among the Soviet Evangelicals* (Edinburgh: Banner of Truth, 1986), p.98.

Chapter 11: The love of money

1. Kidner, *A Time*, p.55.
2. *TIME*, 9 November 1987, p.33.
3. Leaving an inheritance for your children is mandated by Scripture, but God has promised to care for those of his children who have no inheritance from their parents (Ps. 37:25). Furthermore, the parable of the prodigal son (Luke 15:11-24) offers a healthy caution with respect to inheritances and their use and abuse by children.
4. See Larry Burkett, *Your Finances in Changing Times* (Chicago: Moody, 1982), a helpful review of personal finances, including the place of savings.
5. Bridges, *Ecclesiastes*, p.119.
6. W. G. T. Shedd, *Sermons to the Spiritual Man* (London: Banner of Truth, 1972 [1884]), p.374. Shedd was Professor of Systematic Theology in Union Seminary, New York.

Chapter 12: Alternatives

1. Bridges, *Ecclesiastes*, p.119.
2. Eaton, *Ecclesiastes*, p.108.

Chapter 13: Hard experiences

1. Eaton, *Ecclesiastes*, p.109.
2. Rita Nightingale, *Freed for Life* (London: Marshalls, 1982), p.139.
3. Ibid., p.140.
4. James W. Alexander, *Consolation* (New York: Charles Scribner, 1853), p.323.
5. In the Presbyterian system of church government, the 'presbytery' is the regional assembly of congregations within its bounds. Pastors and elders are delegated to this body from their local congregations. Among other things, the presbytery oversees the preparation of men for the pastoral ministry and examines them at regular intervals in their course through seminary.
6. Eaton, *Ecclesiastes*, p.110.

Chapter 14: Clearing hurdles

1. Bridges, *Ecclesiastes*, p.144.
2. Thomas Boston (1676-1732) was a pastor in the Presbyterian Church of Scotland and famous for his role in the 'Marrow controversy' that rocked and revived the Scottish Church. His works are still in print, and his best-known work, *Human Nature in its Fourfold State* is one of the truly great books of Christian doctrine and piety.

Chapter 15: Facing reality

1. Psalm 139:7 refers, of course, to the exact opposite. God has promised to be with his people in all their troubles, wherever they are and for their comfort and preservation.
2. Thomas Manton, *The Complete Works,* vol. 2 (Worthington, Pa: Maranatha, 1975 [1871]), p.102. Manton (1620-77) was a prominent pastor and Bible expositor in England. His works fill twenty-two volumes and comprise a full record of his preaching ministry. J. C. Ryle described these as 'literary gold'.
3. Zophar the Naamithite asks Job, 'Can you fathom [by searching, AV] the mysteries of God? Can you probe the limits of the Almighty?' (Job 11:7). The answer is obvious. Yet man enthrones himself on no more basis than his own empirical interpretation of the world of his senses.
4. Jesus, after his conversation with the woman at the well, takes up this theme with his disciples with the illustration of fields that are ready for harvest (John 4:35-38). God deals with each generation as the farmer does with his harvest. The harvest must be reaped, or the crops will rot where they stand. This is the challenge to every

generation of Christians — to reap God's harvest from their own time and generation.

5. Leupold, *Ecclesiastes*, p.162.

Chapter 16: Wising up

1. Bridges, *Ecclesiastes*, p.173.
2. F. L. Battles comments, in a footnote, on Calvin's use of the same expression in relation to how we are to think of the biblical teaching on predestination. See John Calvin, *Institutes of the Christian Religion*, F. L. Battles, ed. (Philadelphia: Westminster Press, 1960), I1I.XXI.2.
3. Bridges, *Ecclesiastes*, p.175.

Chapter 17: Respect authority!

1. Eaton, *Ecclesiastes*, p.120, no. 1.
2. Canute ruled England from 1016 to 1035. He arrived in England as a pagan Viking raider and died (aged forty) as the Christian King of Denmark, Norway, England, and the Hebrides: 'in the odour of sanctity', according to the historian G. M. Trevelyan. An eleventh-century song celebrated his popularity among his Christian subjects:

> Merry sungen the monkes in Ely
> When Cnut King rowed thereby.
> Row, cnichts, near the land
> And hear we these monkes sing.

3. Hengstenberg, *Ecclesiastes*, p.198.

Chapter 18: Coping with injustice

1. Eaton, *Ecclesiastes*, p.121.
2. Bridges, *Ecclesiastes*, p.206.
3. Ibid, p.207.

Chapter 19: Is there any hope?

1. Scottish schools were then required by law to hold daily

services of worship and provide religious instruction classes, part of the *quid pro quo* for the handover of the hundreds of church schools to the State in 1872.

2. Eaton, *Ecclesiastes*, p.125.

3. In Romans 5:12-21 Paul develops the two themes of sin-condemnation-death (in Adam) and righteousness-justification-life (in Christ) to bring out the meaning of the gospel way of salvation for lost sinners in a fallen world. The juxtaposition between these two themes provides a theological perspective on the conflict of light and darkness for both the individual lives of men and women and the destiny of human history as a whole. Cf. John Murray, *The Epistle to the Romans* (Grand Rapids: Eerdmans, 1968), pp.78-80.

4. Bridges, *Ecclesiastes*, pp.215-16.

5. Robert Leighton, *Commentary on First Peter* (Grand Rapids: Kregel, 1972), p.31.

Chapter 20: Living in hope!

1. Bridges, *Ecclesiastes,* p.219. 'A sinner has no right,' says Bridges, and 'a Christian — supported by Divine strength, favour and consolation has no reason to complain. His treasure includes the promise of all that he wants, in a deep sense of his own unworthiness, and of his Father's undeserved love.'

2. Eaton, *Ecclesiastes,* p.127, notes that 'this almost Pauline touch [in 9:7] is the nearest the Preacher came to a doctrine of justification by faith'.

3. Hengstenberg, *Ecclesiastes*, p.215.

4. Eaton, *Ecclesiastes*, pp.89,128.

5. John Owen, *The Grace and Duty of Being Spiritually Minded*, vol.1 in *The Works of John Owen*, W. H. Goold, ed. (London: Banner of Truth, 1965), p.321.

Chapter 21: You are only human!

1. M. Wilcocks, *I Saw Heaven Opened — The Message of Revelation* (Leicester: Inter-Varsity, 1975], pp.100-102) discusses the significance of God's thunders and trumpets in terms of the limits of his patience with a wicked world.
2. Hengstenberg, *Ecclesiastes*, p.221.

Chapter 22: The heart of folly

1. A. J. P. Taylor, *The First World War* (New York: Penguin, 1965), p.142.
2. Bridges, *Ecclesiastes*, p.237.
3. Quoted by ibid., p.239. George Herbert (1593-1633) is one of England's chief poets. His major work, *The Temple,* is a mystical evocation of Christian spirituality through a poetic description of the church building.
4. Kidner, *A Time*, p.92.
5. Eaton, *Ecclesiastes,* p.136.
6. George Grant, *The Dispossessed: Homelessness in America* (Fort Worth: Dominion Press, 1986), p.34. This masterly and moving account of modern homelessness argues that this problem is the great unrecognized challenge, in the sphere of practical mercy ministry, facing the church today.
7. Eaton, *Ecclesiastes,* p.136.

Chapter 23: Live by faith!

1. The Hebrew *lechem* (bread) is used in Isaiah 28:29 for the grain from which the bread is made. See J. A. Alexander, *The Prophecy of Isaiah* (Grand Rapids: Zondervan, 1974 [1875]), p.459.
2. Bridges, *Ecclesiastes*, p.263.
3. F. N. Lee, *The Covenantal Sabbath* (London: LDOS, 1972), pp.13,75.
4. Eaton, *Ecclesiastes,* p.143.
5. John Flavel, *The Mystery of Providence* (Edinburgh: Banner of Truth, 1976 [1678]), pp.210-11.

6. John W. Keddie, *Scottish Athletics* (Glasgow: SAAA, 1982), p.54. In her biography of Liddell, Sally Magnusson records how it was the Christian witness of Eric Liddell that deeply influenced the Christian faith of track historian John Keddie (this writer's brother, now a minister of the gospel in Scotland). She relates how this led to his involvement in the script-writing for the Liddell character in the movie *Chariots of Fire*. See Sally Magnusson, *The Flying Scotsman* (London: Quartet, 1981), pp.184-85.

Chapter 24: Live joyfully!
1. Hengstenberg, *Ecclesiastes*, p.239.
2. Eaton, *Ecclesiastes*, p.145.
3. Hengstenberg, *Ecclesiastes*, p.242.
4. Eaton, *Ecclesiastes*, p.145.
5. Kidner, *A Time*, p.100.

Chapter 25: Remember your Creator!
1. Eaton, *Ecclesiastes*, pp.147-8.
2. Bridges, *Ecclesiastes*, p.286.
3. Ibid.
4. Cornelis Gilhuis, *Conversations on Growing Older* (Grand Rapids: Eerdmans, 1977), pp.1&19. This wonderful book ought to be read by every young person.
5. The NASB follows the unaccountable rendering of the Septuagint (the Greek Old Testament) to offer 'the caperberry is ineffectual'. The caperberry was, it seems, a stimulant in some use at that time.
6. 'Cryonics' is the process that will allegedly, sometime in the future, revive frozen bodies and give them new lives.
7. Leupold, *Ecclesiastes,* p.282.

NOTES

Chapter 26: Time to respond

1. J. I. Packer, *Knowing God* (Downer's Grove, Ill: Inter-Varsity, 1973), p.94.
2. Ibid., p.92.
3. Ibid., p.94.
4. Ibid., pp.96-97.